MORE SPACE

MORE SPACE

AN INSPIRATIONAL AND PRACTICAL GUIDE TO ADDING MORE SPACE TO YOUR HOME

FAY SWEET

conran
OCTOPUS

contents

First published in 2002 by
Conran Octopus Limited
A part of Octopus Publishing Group
2–4 Heron Quays
London E14 4JP

www.conran-octopus.co.uk

ISBN 1 84091 230 8

Text © Conran Octopus 2002
Design and layout © Conran Octopus 2002

Publishing Director: Lorraine Dickey
Senior Editor: Katey Day
Copy-editor: Lindsay Porter
Index: Richard Bird

Creative Director: Leslie Harrington
Creative Manager: Lucy Gowans
Designer: Alison Fenton

Picture Researcher: Marissa Keating
Location Researchers: Rachel Davies, Sian Lloyd

Production Manager: Adam Smith

The right of Fay Sweet to be identified as the Author of this Work has been asserted by her in accordance with the Copyright, Designs and Patents Act 1988

British Library Cataloguing-in-Publication Data
A catalogue record for this book is available from the British Library

Printed and bound in China

introduction

This is a fascinating time to be writing about homes and architecture and this book was inspired by the hundreds of imaginative and beautiful projects I've visited around the world. The more I see, the more I'm convinced that domestic architecture is enjoying an amazingly creative period, producing homes that are not only stunning to look at, but that are also a pleasure to live in, adding enormously to our quality of life.

I am continually impressed by the skills of architects, who make the most of small spaces, reorganize the layouts of homes to create more comfortable and enjoyable rooms and use even the humblest of materials in clever ways. But of course, very little of this new work would be possible without you – the client. Much of the credit for today's contemporary-style homes must go to the homeowners who have the vision and courage to make changes as well as the confidence to commission and work hand-in-hand with the best designers.

With increasing numbers of us becoming homeowners, property has become one of life's biggest expenses but also an important investment. As everyday work and survival becomes tougher and more stressful, we make greater demands on the home to be a place for solace, for relaxing and recharging. We entertain friends more at home, we have guests to stay more frequently, we may even work from home. As a result of these subtle changes, we use our homes differently from the way our parents used their homes. And this needs to be reflected and accommodated in home design.

So, as the name spells out, this book is about adding to our homes so that the spaces work harder and provide the sort of living areas we really want. Adding more space is nothing new of course, homes have been expanded and adapted to changing needs throughout the centuries. But while our parents generation may have chosen to add space by building a conservatory, or a new bedroom and bathroom extension, the options on offer now are a great deal more exciting.

As you'll see in the following pages, inspiration comes in all shapes and sizes. The ideas for adding more space can be as simple as building a modest timber deck or as complex as a whole new kitchen/dining room extension. Whichever you choose, enjoy your new space.

RIGHT **The asymmetrical shapes and beautiful materials used to create this series of timber-decked terraces demonstrate how contemporary design is synonymous with an imaginative use of space. Small rectangular balconies might have been adequate, but certainly not as exciting.**

inspiration

We all want more space, yet it is a luxury and can be a particularly expensive one at that. Many of us dream of the day when we can expand our homes, add an extension or convert the attic. It takes no effort to imagine how life could be less chaotic and better organized if only we had a bigger living space, room for a home office, an extra bathroom or a guest bedroom.

For most people extra living space has traditionally been acquired by moving house, but if you are happy with where you live, the upheaval and expense of moving can be deeply unappealing. The increasingly popular option is to make the most of the space you already have by extending or adapting it to suit your needs.

Every home has pockets of underused or completely unused space, and this book aims to provide inspiration for making the most of every single centimetre and adding the most useful extra space. Ideas can be drawn from anywhere – from the homes of friends, newly built showhouses, country mansions, hotels or even seaside bathing huts. Get it right and you'll not only be adding to the usefulness and value of your home, you'll also be adding to your quality of life.

LEFT **The luxury of more space enables us to create inspiring areas like this. A glass floor lets light fall into the room below and the transparent bubble chair is the perfect spot for chilling out and enjoying the view.**

1

a brief history

The urge to add more space to our homes is far from a new phenomenon. For centuries people have relished the opportunity to burst through the restrictions imposed by their four walls and push outwards to extend their living space. Throughout history homeowners have added to their properties by building on larders, dairies, laundry rooms, conservatories, annexes, garages and lean-to-extensions – even whole new wings.

ABOVE This is the grand manor of Springhill in County Londonderry, Ireland. The main portion of the house dates from the late seventeenth century, however, it was well into the next century when the owning family decided to add a flourish and built the pair of charming hexagonal side extensions.

RIGHT Rustic stone building forms the heart of this stunning house in Wisconsin. However, despite a tough local housing inspectorate, modern-style wings have been added, one clad in sheet steel, the other in timber, demonstrating the excitement of mixing old and new styles.

These additions were usually conceived and constructed as a result of changed circumstances or fashions – perhaps there was a new child in the family or a new conservatory was the latest in home improvements. It is only recently that people have taken the drastic step of uprooting and moving house when they need more space or want a different style of home. Even until the middle of the twentieth century it was the norm in most countries for families to remain in one area, and often in one house, for generations. The homes in which people were born and raised were regularly subjected to alteration and extension as they were adapted to changing needs.

It has almost always been the case that home additions have gone hand in hand with improving the quality of life. In medieval times in Northern Europe the main room (or hall in grand houses) was the only living space. Here all of daily life was carried out, including cooking, eating, leisure and sleeping. In the following centuries, as life changed and house design grew more sophisticated, homes were divided into rooms for specific activities. Interestingly, extensions were completed without planning laws, and so were built in the style of the day (sometimes with a completely different character to the main house), using the building techniques and materials close to hand. This makes it incredibly rare to find an old house still as it was when first built.

In the grander homes of the past, adding space was often an exciting adventure, exploring the latest architectural design ideas and cutting-edge construction techniques. All too often when we visit grand houses today, the full story of their evolution is rarely told. A country mansion might be described as having been built in the 18th century, but this is likely to be only a portion of the truth. It may also have been extended, remodelled, burned down and rebuilt during the nineteenth and twentieth centuries. Looking around old country mansions it is easy to find additions. Just as the different owners will have bought their own furniture through the ages, so it is almost inevitable that they will have left their mark in the shape of building adaptations and additions. However, because the whole will have acquired an even patina of age, it often takes a fairly sharp eye to spot where the original structure ends and the

ABOVE LEFT This Danish house has grown over the years and the various buildings bear helpful dates – there is a bridge, for example, that bears the date 1336 and may indicate the date of the original building. The section to the right of the tree has the date 1827.

ABOVE Building tree houses dates right back to ancient times. This charming tree house set in an extremely old lime tree can be seen at Pitchford Hall in Shropshire, England. It was constructed in the mid-eighteenth century in the same style as Pitchford Hall.

additions begin. In some buildings, the proud owners helpfully add plaques or inscriptions bearing dates of new additions; elsewhere clues will need to be found. Look out for differences in the shape and style of windows, changes in the roofline, whether brick walls butt up to stone and whether there are changes in the flooring materials. Our forebears felt no pressure or necessity to build extensions in keeping with the style of the original building.

Of course, there were times when rooms were added for entirely practical reasons – to provide more or upgraded space or for an expanding live-in staff, perhaps. However, where there was money there was often also exuberance and in most cases additions to grand houses were made to add a flourish and to impress. There might be a whole new wing for the house, an orangery, a new picture gallery, a chapel, a library or a billiards room to demonstrate the owner's success and refined taste. The expansion of these domestic empires didn't stop at the house – grounds might boast new cart lodges, a gatehouse with clock tower, a summer house or palm house or a folly in the shape of a Classical temple. Many of these new structures were added just for sheer pleasure.

RIGHT **This courtyard is part of Saltram House in Devon, England. The main house was built in the mid-eighteenth century incorporating parts of a Tudor house on the site. Here the Tudor kitchen opens onto the courtyard with the Georgian addition behind.**

more space today

Today we have new and evolving ideas about how we want to live, and this is clearly having an impact on how we add to our homes. The need for a new servants' wing has certainly disappeared into the mists of time – today our concerns are quite different. Among the most powerful influences shaping the contemporary home is our increasingly informal lifestyle and the desire to spend more time outside. Informal suppers with friends have taken over from formal dinners, open-plan living spaces have replaced homes divided into a rigid group of rooms and we want to enjoy decks, gardens and terraces. We have become ever more inventive in the ways in which we blur boundaries between rooms and between indoors and outside.

In addition to this, rising property prices and increasingly dense concentrations of urban homes have meant that many of us now live in smaller spaces than might have been the case even a generation ago.

In smaller homes there is simply no room to be wasted and so we need to think creatively to make the most of every pocket of space. In order to maximize the home's possibilities,

clever new ways are being found to unlock the potential of unused space.

Some of the most exciting recent ideas include entire prefabricated rooms that can be loaded onto the roof of a building and then connected to the home interior by a simple flight of stairs. There are also balconies and whole new rooms that hang off the sides of walls; tiny sun decks built into a roofscape; and glass roofs that open and transform themselves into sky terraces. These new extensions do not only head skyward – there have also been advances in building techniques, including excavating technology that opens up the potential of building below ground. Subterranean extensions are often expensive, but can produce extremely useful new space. Digging downwards has even become one of the few ways to extend properties protected because of their architectural heritage.

LEFT AND ABOVE Rooftop building can produce stunning results and the best city views. Smart property owners are developing this previously unused roofscape, which in real-estate jargon is called 'airspace'. In this project the kitchen and dining area opens onto the timber-decked terrace by pivoting the whole wall of glass. Based on the idea of a garage door, this huge panel of glass opens by flipping up and lying flat against the ceiling.

letting your imagination go

You may already have an idea about the sort of extra space that you would like to add to your home, but don't call the builders just yet. Consider as many options as possible before you make up your mind. While your instinct may be to add an extension that reaches out into the garden, it may turn out that converting an attic actually provides you with a more useful series of spaces that could add considerably to the enjoyment of your home as well as boosting its value.

As you will see from the projects featured in this book some of the most successful, appealing and intriguing extensions are also the most unlikely. Just a small change can sometimes make a big difference – but to make it work, you first need a brilliant idea. For example, by changing the position of the stairway and relocating it, say, in a tower on the back of the house, you could find that the interior becomes a series of uninterrupted spaces.

At the start of any building project, the process should begin with dreams.

Draw ideas from buildings everywhere, whether it's an hotel or a restaurant, a barge or a bank. Look at materials: a glass and steel extension might give you exactly the sort of sun-filled, outward-looking space you desire. Or if you are looking for something more cocoon-like, maybe a timber extension with log-cabin appeal would fit the bill.

As ideas come and go, pin down what sort of extra space you would like. Whether you need a single room or a complete additional storey, think carefully about how the space will be used. Consider whether the interior should feel light and open or sheltered and cosy, and how the space will be finished and decorated.

BELOW **This glass and steel box provides an unusual and refreshing alternative to the timber-framed summerhouse. The all-glass walls make it possible for occupants to be close to nature while also protected from the weather. The roof and base are made from copper and will age to a lovely pale green.**

going wild upstairs

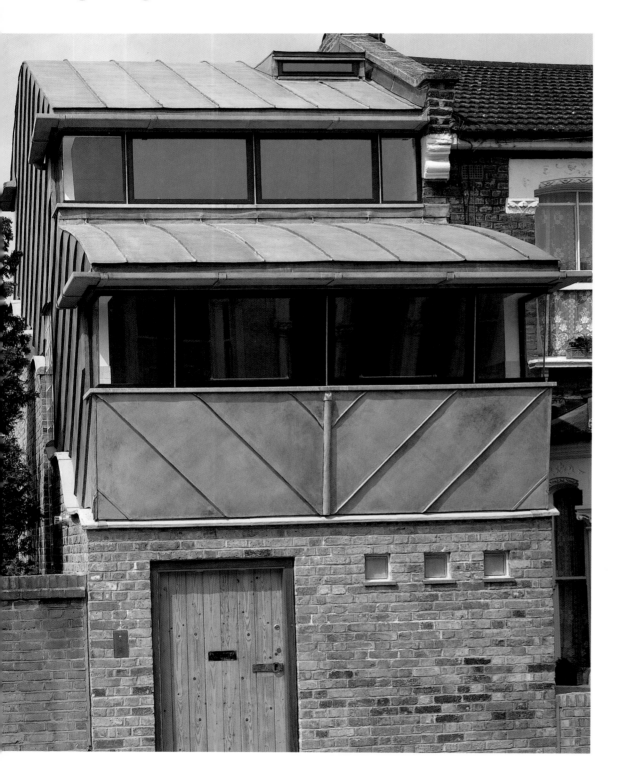

There can be little doubt that the most under-exploited space in any house is an unconverted attic. However, there is more potential lying above our heads than simply a dark and dusty roof space ready and waiting to be transformed into a playroom or den. Take a look up there to see just how much space is readily useful, but then let your imagination run wild. Perhaps there is the opportunity to raise the entire roof to gain valuable height. Depending on the size of the roof and how it has been built, this may not be as crazy as it first seems. Alternatively, it may be possible to add in a dormer window – this is designed to push through the sloping sides of the roof and provide more head space. At its most extreme a dormer window can be added to an entire side of the roof – incorporate floor-to-ceiling windows along its length and you have a generous, well-lit additional room. Other options for this area might be to remove all, or a portion, of the roof tiles and replace them with glass – add a sliding roof window so that light and fresh air flow into the space.

If the roof space proves to be too small or difficult to transform, it can still be used to enhance the rooms below. Remove the ceiling in bedrooms and open them up to the rafters, insulate the sloping sides and fit roof-lights and

LEFT **This award-winning modern studio-house was built in 1998 in London, England. The architect used copper to clad the new extension and so gave a traditional material a modern architectural twist.**

your bedrooms will become lighter and gain a greater sense of space.

The quality of a converted attic space is often underestimated – given plenty of windows this can become one of the best rooms in the entire house. It is quiet and removed from the hustle and bustle of street life below, it is blessed with natural sunlight, and if properly insulated it will remain at a comfortable temperature – boosted in the winter by warm air rising from the rooms below.

For those feeling really adventurous, work on an attic can lead to the imaginative remodelling of the entire house. Since the quality of the upper spaces fits exactly with our desire for natural light and tranquillity, this could be the moment to rethink how you use the home and turn the whole place upside down by relocating bedrooms and bathrooms to the lower levels of the house. Here natural light is in shorter supply than upstairs, but most people prefer to sleep in a bedroom free of bright sunlight and bathrooms can be stylish and comfortable with little or no natural light. Keep higher floors for bright, open living space.

ABOVE The old timbers of this 1888 warehouse in Antwerp have been stripped back and exposed to provide the frame for a contemporary two-storey home. Exciting details include the bed 'box' which appears to hover in space, but which is actually suspended from the eaves. It is reached via a delightfully simple oak stairway.

going underground

Basements have languished in the dark for too long. So it has been a delight to see how the skills of a good architect can utterly transform our preconceptions of subterranean living. In recent years there has been an astonishing range of projects demonstrating the potential of these once-unpromising spaces. By adding extra windows, glass doors and other devices for introducing more natural light, basement flats have been opened out into gardens, low-ceilinged cellars have been excavated and waterproofed to make additional useful living spaces and coal holes have been converted into kitchens, bathrooms and mini gyms. Occasionally, entire houses have been built underground.

A sizeable international interest in underground homes developed during the second half of the 20th century – not least because this form of building was recognized as environmentally sound. It is estimated that at least 150,000 underground homes exist in the USA and Canada. There has even emerged an international special-interest group called the Earth Sheltering Association, which is dedicated to promoting the building and understanding of underground homes. The advantages are many. In terms of construction, underground homes can be hidden in green landscapes, they can cost less to build than conventional homes, they require little maintenance and they have a long life expectancy. In terms of aesthetics, they are sympathetic to landscaping, can be designed with wonderful light-filled internal courtyards, and, if set into a gently sloping site, have great views. In terms of running costs they are well insulated and maintain a steady temperature with no draughts; the overall energy consumption can be as low as 25 per cent of a standard house of the same size.

LEFT **A huge new living room has been created in this London house by excavating the garden. Some 300 tonnes of earth were removed and around 79 m² (850 ft²) was added to the property.**

RIGHT **Glass walls and glass balustrading help draw light into the lower floors of this home. The glass wall lets light into the room below and makes a feature of the cute car stored on a hydraulic platform.**

inside out

ABOVE **Taking inspiration from Japanese temples and English cottages, this is a highly unusual pool house. The design involves a daring collision of old-world thatch and crisp glass modernism.**

RIGHT **Now that the garden has become an extension of our living space, architects and designers have devised ingenious ways of blurring the boundaries between inside and out. In this home the timber-decked veranda wraps round much of the building to provide a transitional inside/outside space. The long drop blinds provide shade in the heat of the day and protection against winds.**

The ways in which we extend our homes outwards change constantly. In the recent past, the conservatory has ruled. This sparkling glass room has drawn inspiration from such tremendous feats of architecture and construction as the Crystal Palace built for the Great Exhibition of 1851 in London, England.

In the 18th century, as interest grew in exotic plants, protective plant houses were built to accommodate them. In northern Europe many great country-house owners took delight in building on glass structures, which they called orangeries. As the decades passed this once-great luxury of the extremely rich became translated into the conservatory of the wealthy merchant classes. The spaces were used as sun rooms, a place to sit and read or perhaps take tea.

Today, all this has changed. The conservatory is no longer required to conserve and there is rarely a potted plant or cane chair in sight. There are, of course, many types of extension, but the most popular by far is still that extra light and airy space; a room that opens from the house onto a deck or garden, preferably with floor-to-ceiling doors and windows that can be folded or slid aside. By dissolving the boundary between inside and out we have at last achieved the great Modernist ideal of being protected from the extremes of weather and yet free to enjoy the pleasures of nature. But today this room has to work hard. In the modern home we can't afford to waste space. We expect our glass extensions to become a focus of family life. Here, finishes tend to be natural and simple such as timber or stone floors and pale walls. In the middle might sit a refectory-style table with plenty of chairs, providing a place for family meals throughout the day as well as a place to entertain friends to big informal lunches and suppers. Our homes may be closed and protected where they face onto the street, but where they face the garden they are open and extrovert, letting us make the most of our own piece of Eden.

far out and fantastic

ABOVE **The simplest structures can provide a welcome resting place in any garden or landscape. This hexagonal timber boathouse makes an idyllic place to pause and enjoy the beauty and tranquillity of the scenery.**

RIGHT **Venice Beach, California, is noted for its wild and experimental architecture and this look-out post is no exception. The small cabin on stilts is reminiscent of a tree house, a crow's nest or perhaps the bridge of a boat.**

Children adore fantasy places whether a tree house or a den, the corner of a shed or a tent. Here, they can give their imagination free rein and create a world away from grown-up rules. Many adults also delight in a space to dream, to contemplate and to be ourselves away from the pressures and responsibilities of everyday life. Some people will find solace and rejuvenation in listening to or playing music, meditating, writing, reading or

pursuing hobbies. The spaces don't have to be for solitary use either – a garden shed readily converts into a mini cinema, or a garage can be transformed into a small theatre. Of course, most people don't own a lake on which they can build their own boathouse or a mountainside plot for a log-cabin retreat, but it is precisely these sorts of buildings that provide inspiration for the more modest versions we may build for ourselves.

With imagination and even very limited resources it remains entirely possible for most of us to make personalized spaces – perhaps inside the home, but most successfully outside in the garden or even on the roof.

The skill in creating a fantasy place comes from starting with your own dream. On visits to large country estates you are almost certain to have seen shell-covered grottoes, summerhouses and scaled-down temples – an entire collection of fantastic buildings dreamed up by previous generations. Think back to childhood and the places you enjoyed; think of holiday retreats, making a hideaway in an upturned boat, or seaside and fun-fair architecture. All these places share a number of elements in common – they are informal, often built using inexpensive materials, fairly basic in design and sometimes quite temporary. They might incorporate canvas, lightweight screens, sheets of Perspex or galvanized iron.

A large part of the charm of these structures is that they can be rough around the edges and built by unskilled enthusiasts. The dictates of exacting building standards do not have to apply – a wall can be made from a piece of plywood. A door can be a cotton sheet or an entire structure can be made from a piece of canvas slung between trees. Here is the ideal spot for lazy afternoon reading in the shade, a barbecue or a quiet picnic.

future follies

You may be forgiven for thinking that the era of folly building is long past. However, it is an area of fantasy architecture that continues to thrive. The term folly was probably first coined back in the 13th century to describe a Welsh castle, but it was then used in a Latin context. More recently the word was used in the USA in 1746 in reference to an enormous and lavishly built house used by the owner for just one month each year. Today the term refers to a huge variety of decorative but usually impractical buildings. Follies can be found all over the world but they are most celebrated in Britain where eccentricity is firmly embedded in the national character.

This building type is intentionally useless, but the structures do perform the function of raising a smile and raising the spirits. They also provide plenty of inspiration for anyone embarking on an unusual building for the sheer delight of it – though planning authorities may not always agree.

ABOVE This is a contemporary interpretation of the Scottish 'sitooterie' – a colloquial term for a structure to sit out in. Called the Music Sitooterie it is an arena for performing and listening to music. The canopy is formed by an inflated silver disc supported on three stainless steel V-shaped legs.

OPPOSITE Set in a woodland this folly or 'sitooterie' is based on a Romanesque church. The small scale building made from wood provides views of the trees and is finished in a skin of colourful, sparkling metal discs.

going up

It is only during the last few decades that we have really begun to appreciate and experiment with the potential of the architectural space over our heads. As many homeowners have witnessed, attics and roofs can be transformed into appealing new rooms that are quiet and full of light. Much of this work has been fuelled by rising property prices and increasing population density in cities; as houses and apartments get smaller, so we want to make the most of every centimetre of spare space.

As the following pages show, there are many more options available than just a straightforward attic conversion. Architects and designers continue to pull out all the stops to produce incredibly imaginative schemes, often from utterly unpromising circumstances.

The twin basics of good safe access and natural sunlight are the keys to transforming this elevated, tranquil space. Along with attic conversions and the introduction of mezzanine levels, the most innovative new ideas include constructing a whole extra storey, add-on prefabricated structures, creating sky gardens, adding luxurious hot tubs or perhaps just hanging up a simple canvas awning to mark out a seating area and provide dappled shade.

LEFT **The most wonderful light can be discovered by opening up attic spaces. Here the large rooflights draw in a huge slice of light, making this an ideal home office.**

mezzanine floors

The addition of a mezzanine level can be a visually exciting and extremely useful device for gaining some precious extra floor space. Architects and designers have really excelled themselves in recent projects.

In older traditional-style houses, clever ways of dividing tall hallways have included adding a sleeping deck or storage space over a cloakroom, or inserting a small platform over the stairwell. In large houses and mansion blocks, tall reception rooms have been divided horizontally to make a single self-contained apartment. Often this is achieved by creating a compact kitchen and bathroom tucked under a sleeping platform, thus leaving the largest part of the room as a generous open space.

In modern warehouse and factory conversions, designers have used the mezzanine level as a way of keeping the luxurious sense of space and light often provided by very tall windows. Set back from the exterior wall, the mezzanine level is most often used as a bedroom or office. Glass is often used in order to let natural light flow through these spaces, perhaps for balustrading or even floors.

LEFT A mezzanine level can provide useful extra floor space. In this apartment the extra floor – viewed from its twin mezzanine – is put to good use as a large, light-filled office.

RIGHT This one-bedroom apartment received much-needed floor space by the addition of a glass-floored mezzanine living area above the kitchen. The laminated glass floor panel lets in light from above.

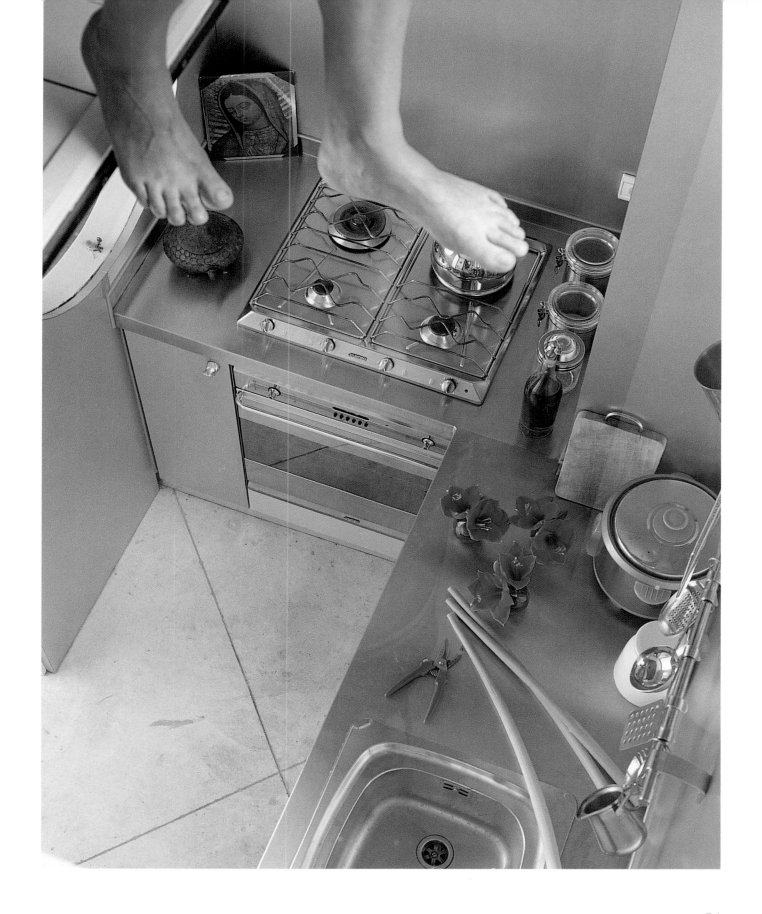

There are countless ways of adding this precious extra layer of mezzanine space, but practical considerations must come first. It is essential that your room is tall enough to take the addition of an extra floor. The maximum headroom height depends on how you plan to use the new space. If your dream is to add a large extra platform, then there must be a ceiling height of at least 2 m (6½ ft) at each level below and above the new mezzanine. This is vital where you need to stand upright either under or on the mezzanine floor. Building regulations differ from country to country so it is worth checking with your local authority, but for the sake of comfort, a height of 2 m (6½ ft) is the absolute minimum. Remember to add the depth of the new mezzanine floor itself to your calculations.

To gain additional height, it may even be possible to excavate and drop the ground floor level. If the new mezzanine is planned for the top floor of a building, you may be able to remove a ceiling and open the space to the rafters.

However, if the plan is to add something as simple as a platform for sleeping or a small home office, you may be able to compromise on height. Even in fairly modest-sized homes, sleeping platforms have long been a

RIGHT **A clever, lightweight structure built in metal was inserted into this building to make a sleeping platform. The slender mezzanine ensures that it is still possible to appreciate the beauty of the stone and brick archway.**

feature of children's bedrooms. Plenty of furniture-makers have made platforms with a child's desk and wardrobe beneath and this idea can easily be translated for adults. The access ladder or stair is vitally important and should be designed to be as comfortable and as safe as possible. Steep ladders with narrow steps are miserable to use and can entirely detract from the bonus of adding a mezzanine.

Further practical considerations include whether the main structure can support the weight of an additional level. Will it rest on the floor or would it require additional support from the walls? Take advice on this from a structural engineer. Consider whether natural light is important for the new level. If it is to be used for sleeping, then a window is probably not required, but if you plan to work there at your computer, some natural light will certainly make the space more appealing. Add plenty of lights and electrical sockets and make sure the edge of the platform is adequately and safely balustraded.

As for aesthetics, think about how big the new mezzanine will be and how it will fit into the existing space. Try to resist the temptation to add a vast extra floor – it really shouldn't dominate the whole room.

LEFT **In most cases the design of a mezzanine level is finished with a waist-high wall or balustrading. This unusual design incorporates a low-level horizontal window looking into the space below.**

finding space in the attic

Convert your attic and you could add as much as 30 per cent to your home's floor space. Add light, stairs and insulation and you could create the most appealing space in the house for about the same cost as a new car.

If you are lucky enough to be the owner of an unconverted attic, then the first step to realizing your full property potential is to grab a ladder and go up and have a look inside. In older and traditionally built homes, roofs were constructed in a way that makes attics easy to convert. Ideal roof trusses should be a large upside-down 'V' shape with little in the middle to obstruct the space. A worst-case scenario is the modern style of truss – often an 'A' shape with timbers running right across the middle of the room. Fortunately, even in the latter case, it is often possible to re-brace the main rafters, but before embarking on such an exercise consult a structural engineer to make sure the extra expense is worth investing.

Another vital consideration is roof height. If you can only just stand in the apex of the space, you effectively have nothing but a corridor running through the middle of the room. You will need at least 2 m (6 ½ ft) height and width. If the roof line doesn't provide that sort of space, all is not lost – in many attics it is possible to add a dormer window that will raise up one side of the roof to make a horizontal extension. In some situations the entire roof can be raised to provide those vital extra centimetres of height and width.

ABOVE The complex junction of roof beams and supports makes an interesting sculptural shape in this converted space. The sloping ceiling of the alcove is almost tent-like and encloses the cosy sleeping area.

LEFT Here a once-dingy attic has been transformed into a tranquil living space drenched in sunlight. The ceiling height is fairly low making it possible to stand upright only in the central area, but as a sitting room it works perfectly well.

case study – lofty ambitions

The unusual choice of metal sheeting to enclose this new attic bathroom was entirely appropriate, since the converted industrial building in which it stands used to be a metalworking factory. The building was used for producing the machines that make domestic washing powder and, because of its proximity to the city centre, was ideal for converting into loft apartments.

To complement the big, open-plan, sun-drenched interiors, the architect devised the bathroom as a small, self-contained pod. It was felt that a separate room would have spoiled the sense of openness and would have interfered with the great views through the space. Corrugated, galvanized steel was chosen to separate the space, partly to echo the architectural heritage of the building, but also because the material would help to reflect light. The reflective surface also creates the illusion of reducing the structure's size.

The bathroom is a simple but effective structure; it is built from hoops of MDF, which act as the framework. The corrugated sheets were then screwed onto the frame. At either end there is an MDF wall with a door and small porthole window. The space inside is divided into two areas – one for the lavatory with its own entrance, the other for the bath and a

THE BRIEF: To design a compact bathroom that maintains a sense of light and space in this attic apartment, while also echoing the building's industrial origins.

THE SOLUTION: A freestanding metal-clad bathroom 'hut' was fitted into the space under the sloping eaves.

pair of simple stainless steel washbasins which have been set into the top of grey PVC columns. Because the hot-water boiler is placed on the floor below the pressure was sufficient to dispense with the need for water pumps.

In converting spaces in the upper floors of a building, a major consideration is how you will gain access. In this case there was generous space to accommodate a stair from the floor below. However in converting the attic of a traditional house, it is important to work out if there is room on the floor below to accommodate a new stairway. Perhaps it can rise from the landing, you may be able to borrow space from a bedroom, or add a separate stairway to the side of the house. An architect will be able to advise you whether or not your project is technically and economically feasible.

The conversion has exposed and celebrated the character of this handsome industrial structure wherever possible. At this top-floor level for example, the interesting web of steel roof-bracing still remains on

RIGHT **The industrial aesthetic is a powerful theme in this converted workshop building. The skin of the bathroom pod is corrugated metal sheeting fixed to the hooped frame. The shiny metal of the walls is picked up and echoed in the pair of stainless steel basins.**

LEFT **The bathroom pod sits to one side of the apartment under a section of sloping roof and opposite the big rooflights. The pod's end wall and door are made from sheet MDF.**

show. However, the first step to making this a habitable apartment was to add a new concrete panel floor – in its former life the workshop had tall open spaces to accommodate the metalworking machinery.

Other important elements of the conversion included fitting large aluminium-frame double-glazed windows, which are highly thermally efficient and allow in generous amounts of sunlight. High levels of insulation around 12 cm (5 in) thick were fitted into the sloping roof. The interiors have been finished as simply as possible.

Some people may find that the bathroom structure is a little too simple. It is quite lightweight, which means that it is easily supported by the concrete floor, but because the walls are constructed from of a single thickness of pressed steel the bathroom unfortunately lacks soundproofing and therefore privacy. This problem could easily be solved however, by fixing a layer of insulation to the inside of the corrugated sheeting and then adding another finish on the inside of the hoops – either sheet steel again or perhaps a smooth ply and plaster lining.

FLOORPLAN
1 living
2 bathroom
3 lavatory
4 sleeping

RIGHT **The shiny corrugated metal sheeting that wraps the bathroom pod shimmers in the sunlight from windows fitted into the roof above the bed. The web of roof braces are left exposed as a reminder of the building's industrial heritage.**

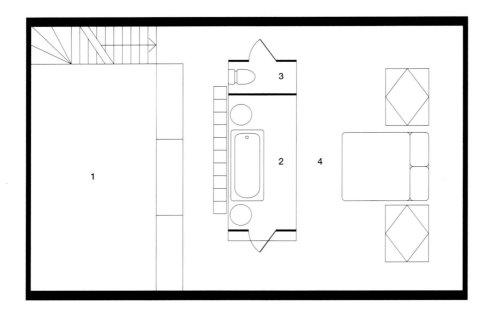

the sky's the limit

For those looking for something more than a straightforward attic conversion, there are plenty of exciting options. Where it is not possible or desirable to extend the roof or add a roof terrace, there are ways of opening up the attic space by introducing more light through windows. New glass technology and construction techniques now make it possible to blur the boundaries between inside and out at roof level.

There are many design routes to take, depending on the result you want to achieve. It is possible to remove fairly small portions of the roof and add dormer windows, or remove larger portions and add big sliding or upward-lifting sheets of glass. You could even strip off the entire roof and replace it with a glazed canopy. Glass is extremely heavy and expensive, so following this path will almost inevitably cost more than an ordinary attic conversion, but the end result will have an invaluable 'wow' factor.

Remember that extra sunlight will generate extra heat from the sun's rays. The light can be harnessed in photovoltaic panels to produce clean electricity and help contribute to the home's energy-efficiency. Photovoltaics use light-sensitive silicon cells to convert light directly into electricity. There are now systems available that suspend the cells in a laminated glass sheet and create a dappled fall of light. Another option is to use glass that has been given a transparent reflective coating that allows light through but filters out the extremes of heat.

LEFT The conversion of this attic meant raising the roof to gain useful head height. Folding doors lead to a small outdoor terrace with glass balustrading for unhindered views.

ABOVE The entire roof was replaced with
sheet glass in this dazzling project. The roof
incorporates four frameless double-glazed
units with a glass ridge beam and rafters.

a room with a view

If you need more space but don't want to move, building upwards to add an extra storey can be one of the most viable forms of extension. It is a great solution if you don't have a garden to house an extension, and an even better idea if you do but want to avoid encroaching on valuable garden space.

Adding an additional storey to your home is different from converting an attic. It is not just about making the most of existing roof space, it is about adding a whole new floor (or even two) of usable space, while possibly also keeping an attic. The most successful versions of this type of enterprise are those where the extra storey is fully integrated into the home, and where the flow of rooms and internal sequence of spaces has been carefully thought through. In one recent city-centre project a two-storey home was raised to a full four storeys, plus attic, to match the size of similar homes in the neighbourhood. The finished project achieved the desired effect of making the new four-storey house look entirely at home with its neighbours; from the outside it is impossible to tell that extra storeys have been added.

Practical concerns begin with making sure that the structure of the building can carry the weight of an additional storey. In such a big project an architect and structural engineer will be key players. For many homes, the foundations could need extra support, so you may have to consider whether expensive underpinning work would still leave the project financially viable.

LEFT The play of sunlight in rooftop spaces is highly seductive. Here light is brought in through rooflights and windows and bounces around the white-painted walls.

BELOW A series of new structures was added to the roof of this converted industrial building. Top floor apartments don't only benefit from having the additional sunny rooms, they also have lovely roof terraces.

FAR LEFT Even a small lean-to extension can add valuable extra space to the home. This simple roof-level structure houses a neat home office.

Once the calculations are done and the project seems realistic, you will probably need to apply for planning permission: it will be up to neighbours and planning officials to decide whether the scheme is acceptable.

The challenge of adding extra storeys to converted industrial buildings has often been met by creating rooftop structures. These are often made from the same materials as the building below, perhaps finished in matching roofing material, but also sometimes built in lighter materials that avoid adding too much weight to the roof. Very often these new additions are set back from the edge of the roof to ensure that they don't interfere with the proportions of the existing building, making it look top heavy.

roof pavilions

The roof pavilion is a fairly new breed of home extension. It is born from our recent interest in pushing at the boundaries of our homes and bursting through walls, floors and now the roof to explore and exploit every pocket of space. Where it is not possible to convert an attic or add a heavyweight, full-scale additional storey, the roof pavilion can be as tranquil and full of light as other rooftop spaces.

Roof pavilions are often made in lightweight materials and feature large expanses of glass to make the most of views and sunlight. As with any extension they can be custom-made to meet your specifications, but you

could also consider using a prefab. This is a relatively new but extremely successful way of building onto the roof. In many cities it is occasionally possible to see cranes lifting prefabricated structures onto the top of buildings. The new room is usually a factory-made product. Some companies produce simply finished empty spaces, while others can make a bespoke interior right down to the marble-clad bathroom, plus all the electrical circuitry and plumbing in place ready to 'plug-in' to the main building. This type of addition works extremely well on mansion blocks of flats or converted industrial buildings where there is a strong, flat roof. However, there are prefab extensions made to fit into roofs of all sorts. In the case of a tiled pitched roof, the tiles will be removed and space cleared for the new prefab room; once it has been lifted into place, the old tiles can be replaced around the new addition.

This type of prefab addition is not for everyone, however: the luxury, pre-fitted modules can weigh as much as 14 tonnes and your roof may not be able to support the weight. You may also find that the preparatory works and cost of the module are beyond your budget. However, the advantages are obvious – the space can be finished exactly to your specifications, the modules can be fitted in a day or two and it is a way of avoiding all the mess and disturbance associated with traditional building works.

ABOVE **To enjoy the views and new garden being created on this rooftop, the architect added a small sunroom with big sliding doors. Particularly appealing details include the sound system – with invisible speakers set into the walls – that has been incorporated into the room.**

LEFT **This lightweight rooftop structure is reminiscent of a greenhouse. The all-round glazing makes the most of the sunlight and the structure is strongly braced to strengthen it against gusts of wind.**

FAR LEFT **The exaggerated slope of this roof was a requirement of the local planning department, who wanted to be sure that this new extension could not be seen from the street. The rooftop pavilion is built from a mahogany frame clad in copper and the floor is covered with rubber tiles.**

The lighter form of roof pavilion shares an ancestry with the greenhouse. Aerial shots of city centres reveal fascinating roofscapes dotted with tiny patches of green, pots of carefully tended plants, flower-festooned sundecks and even the occasional plant-filled greenhouse or conservatory. The human instinct to make contact with the soil remains apparently undiminished – is even sharpened – despite being several storeys above ground.

These aerial structures are often made using a slender wood or steel frame filled with glass panes, just as you would see on a greenhouse at ground level. There are, of course, contemporary interpretations of this type of building and where weight and flexibility are a concern, the glazing can be replaced with modern materials such as translucent polycarbonate sheeting. You will need to think carefully about the orientation of such a building. In the northern hemisphere a glassy south-facing extension will catch the sun's strongest rays and will remain warm even on wintery days. While this is fine – even desirable – for most of the year, it means the interior can become extremely hot in summer months. Where plants are being grown, the heat may become unbearable and so it can be a good idea to build in some form of screening and/or ventilation. East- or west-facing structures will be less hot and north-facing additions will remain coolest of all.

With such lightweight structures it is absolutely vital that they are fixed firmly in place, and that the fixings can withstand the impact of fairly powerful gusts of wind. It is also a good idea to make sure that they are placed in the shelter of other buildings or structures on the roof, which can offer some protection against extremes of weather.

As with all roof buildings, before you begin work, take time to check that the construction materials and sections of the building can be transported up to the roof level. In many cases you may find that you face restrictions imposed by narrow stairs: in which case the only realistic, but sometimes risky, option is to investigate whether the materials can be hoisted either by crane or rope and pulley up the building's side.

LEFT This unusual rooftop greenhouse has been slotted onto a small roofspace. It is given protection from bad weather and winds by being fitted right up against a wall.

RIGHT This contemporary-style rooftop conservatory was built on a modest budget. It is made with simple materials – lightweight polycarbonate sheeting and a braced softwood frame. The skin has been designed to flex slightly when buffeted by the wind.

case study – artist's lightbox

It is no surprise that maximizing natural light was a key element in the brief for this artist's apartment. The client wanted a space that was 'clean and calm' and which 'retained as much light and space as possible'.

The apartment was bought as an empty shell and then fitted out by an architect. The bedroom was to be accommodated in a rooftop steel and glass pavilion, which left the entire area below as a seamless open-plan living space. This elegant sleeping pavilion doubles as a 'lightbox', enabling vast amounts of natural sunlight to flow down into the space below. The pavilion is curtain- and blind-free so that the flow of natural light is uninterrupted; so, too, are the amazing city rooftop views.

The pavilion has been kept as simple and elemental as possible – it is not fitted with electric lighting, except for a single light-fitting under the bed, which gives an unusual spread of light at floor level. However, even without this switched on, the pavilion still works as a lightbox at night, with artificial light from the living area below reflecting off the ceiling. To make sure light can move unimpeded through all the spaces, there is an open-tread stair leading to the sleeping area which concludes in a glass bridge, lit from below by powerful industrial lamps. A simple sandblasted glass balustrade

THE BRIEF: A clean and calm interior that maximizes light and space.

THE SOLUTION: A simple open-plan space that draws in natural light through a 'lightbox' roof pavilion.

shields the bed from the room below. In its peaceful elevated setting, the bed sits on a pale American white-oak floor. The floor-to-ceiling double glazing of the pavilion links inside and out, so the sleeping area becomes part of the peaceful roof garden.

The architect designed all the furniture in the apartment with the exception of the dining chairs. The fascination with light continues on the lower level where the sitting-area sofas are fitted with casters and lights beneath. This glow of artificial light makes the furniture appear to hover just above the floor and adds intriguing lighting into the room.

LOWER LEVEL FLOORPLAN
1 study
2 lavatory
3 shower
4 kitchen
5 dining
6 living
7 terrace

UPPER LEVEL FLOORPLAN
8 bamboo screens
9 roof lights
10 glass bridge
11 void
12 sleeping
13 roof terrace

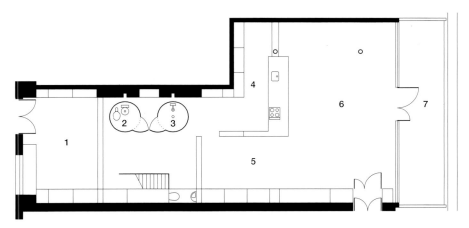

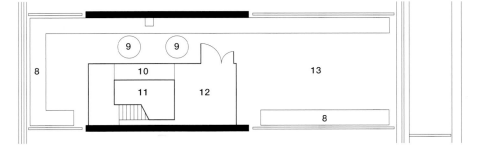

ABOVE Artificial and natural light are an important factors in this apartment for an artist. The architect has built in an unusual lighting system under the living room furniture and beyond this it is possible to see one of the illuminated bathroom pods.

LEFT The rooftop pavilion at night with light reflecting up from the floor below. Cut from the decking outside are the twin circles that form the top of the bathroom pods.

Along with cascades of light brought into the apartment through the glass pavilion, light from the roof is also drawn down into the space below through two unusual, sculptural glass pods that sit in the living space. The sunlight inside the cylinders falls as two perfect shafts of illumination through a pair of circular holes cut out of the iroko roof decking and finished with glass. The glass pods are tailor-made from toughened glass, which has been sandblasted and rubbed with white powder paint to make it more opaque and to provide privacy for those inside. One pod encloses a lavatory while the other contains a shower and washbasin. With the curved doors of both pods fully opened, the two spaces become linked. It is an economic use of space, has avoided the necessity to divide up the living area into separate rooms and provides a highly unusual form of lighting. During the daytime the pods are illuminated by natural sunlight and at night they are lit by recessed ceiling lighting. The floor beneath the pods is raised above the sitting-area level to accommodate the plumbing and also to provide some interesting internal landscaping, creating a subtle sense of separation from the dining and living areas. The client says that both natural and artificial lighting in the space has been particularly successful and sometimes, during restful evenings, they have found the light from the glowing bathroom pods to be the only illumination necessary.

LEFT Looking down from the top of the stairs leading from the sleeping pavilion into the heart of the apartment, it is possible to see how the open spaces let light flood in.

ABOVE This view through the apartment takes in the bathroom pods and the floor-to-ceiling windows beyond. Above is the glass floor of the rooftop sleeping pavilion.

living the highlife

ABOVE **A flat rooftop has been transformed into an elegant and inviting dining terrace. The rich tile pattern and series of huge lanterns make this an alluring place to spend a warm evening.**

In our quest to make the best possible use of any spare space, the flat roof has been seized upon as an ideal extension to the living space. Even without the addition of pavilions or whole new solid structures, the roof can be transformed into an additional outside 'room'. In city-centre apartments, this roof area can take the place of a garden, making it an ideal venue for entertaining friends or simply sitting out and enjoying fresh air and sunshine.

As with any work to be carried out on a roof, there is a list of practicalities to be checked before the project can start. First you must make sure that the structure can withstand the additional weight. Even the addition of a wooden deck may be too much for a

roof designed for providing shelter from rain, but not for carrying half a tonne of timber and six people. The advice of a structural engineer is essential. The next step is to make sure that the access to the roof is safe – a solid flight of steps is a much better idea than a ladder. Make sure the terrace edges are correctly balustraded – check with local planners to find out what height of balustrading is required by law and whether you require a solid barrier or if railings would be sufficient.

Waterproofing will be your next concern. Presumably the roof was watertight before your plans to make changes, but new building works may call for an additional waterproof membrane. Check that the whole

area will be able to drain quickly after heavy rainfall and take care to keep drainage channels clear.

Then comes the fun – deciding on finishes and materials. Your choice will depend on the style of space you want to create. Decking is extremely popular: the best-quality timber ages attractively to reach a soft, silvery-grey finish and requires little maintenance. Stone and ceramic tiles are other beautiful options. Again, they should require little maintenance apart from occasional re-grouting and washing in winter to remove traces of moss, which can make the surface slippery and dangerous. Areas covered with small pebbles add attractive colour and textural contrast to expanses of smooth wood, stone or tile.

TOP An interesting combination of materials makes this a stylish city roof terrace. The disc of timber decking – ideal for a dining table and chairs, is surrounded by small pebbles and partly framed by trough planters finished in sheet aluminium.

ABOVE Even a small terrace can be made into a haven of peace. This contemporary-style area is finished with timber decking and features shaped box trees in huge square metal pots.

head in the clouds

ABOVE A gently bubbling hot tub is the height of rooftop luxury. Many people enjoy their tubs all year round, but before you consider investing in one, it is vital to check practicalities such as roof strength.

RIGHT Less expensive than a hot tub, the inside/outside shower can be fun and also luxurious. However, to be sure of success, make sure that hot water at a good pressure can be fed to the shower head.

For growing numbers of people, the hot tub has become the height of luxury. If you have a terrace or space for a roof deck and you are looking to incorporate a real feature, then an outdoor hot tub is a spectacular addition. In many new urban development projects, the rooftop hot tub has become one of the selling points of upmarket penthouse apartments. It provides an idyllic place to wind down at the end of the day

and soothe away the stresses of working and family life. Of course, you can incorporate a hot tub in a garden or elsewhere inside the home, such as a basement, but there is something extra-special about sitting in hot frothy water out in the open, especially with a great view of the stars.

As might be imagined there are some serious issues to take into account. Any roofscape additions to historic buildings in conservation areas will require planning permission. Of equal importance is whether your roof is strong enough to carry the enormous weight of a large tub full of water. Even a modest-sized tub of 1.2 m (4 ft) across will carry 900 litres (200 gallons) of water and could weigh upwards of 1 tonne. A tub capable of accommodating six people comfortably will need to be 1.8 m (6 ft) across and might weight in at a very substantial 2–3 tonnes.

Along with the matter of structural strength comes the services – do you have an electrical supply and the capacity to get water to the roof level? It is fairly safe to assume that since the roof can cope with rainfall, then it can also cope with possible leakage from a tub. Make sure that you have roof access large enough to raise the tub to the required level – many manufacturers sell their products as a kit of parts, so they have to be carried piece by piece upstairs and then assembled in situ. As ever, if in doubt consult a structural engineer.

If your taste and space is more modest, taking a shower at roof level can be a luxurious and invigorating experience, too. It will be considerably less expensive and less troublesome to install and maintain than a hot tub, and makes showering a real treat if there is a view. In very built-up areas, don't forget that if you can see out, someone else will be able to see in. A small porthole window in a solid wall might be a better choice than a transparent cubicle.

rooftop pools

ABOVE **This serene scene is made possible by creating a fairly shallow pool on the rooftop. The dining deck reaches out across the water so that diners can enjoy the reflections and lapping sounds of the pool.**

RIGHT **A rooftop swimming pool really is for the rock-star rich, but increasing numbers of people are finding ways of incorporating more modest plunge pools and tubs into the roofscape. Here the pool is surrounded by a timber sun deck and can be accessed via the apartment's bathroom.**

For most of us, being able to walk out of the bedroom and into a warm rooftop pool is the stuff of dreams, but why not start planning for the day when dreams come true?

It may at first seem counterintuitive to put a big pool of water on top of a building; the mind immediately conjures up images of disaster, with thousands of litres of water cascading down through the floors. However, it is something we have all lived with for at least a century. In just about every home with hot water, there is a water tank in the roof, and countless hotels

have placed a pool and health spa right at the top of the building. The high-level pool has also become a feature of many new apartment developments. Even in the 1950s, the Swiss architect Le Corbusier included a children's paddling pool on the roof of his famous tower block, l'Unité d'Habitation, in Marseille. Interestingly, he also included outdoor picnic areas, a running track, a gym and even an outdoor cinema – the roofscape is more like a public park than the top of a tower block. As might be expected, the secret of getting it right with large or small pools is perfect waterproofing. This really is a job for a specialist. Draw up a shortlist of potential companies, try and find similar projects to look at and research any possible drawbacks.

A more modest version of the swimming pool is the shallow ornamental pool. The same attention to waterproofing is, of course, essential – any water held on top of a building should be kept in place with a thick, impermeable and flexible membrane. The plasticized material will have a limited life so follow the manufacturer's guidelines and replace it when recommended.

The appeal of water is undeniable – witness the enormous craze for incorporating water features in our gardens – so a pool is always a welcome addition as a cool foil to a sundeck, or, more poetically, as a surface for reflecting the surrounding structures and the sky.

chill-out tents and temporary structures

ABOVE A simple sheet of canvas is stretched between four poles and tethered to the roof to make a patch of shade away from the intense summer sun.

RIGHT Here is a more sophisticated version of the awning shown above. In this design cigar-shaped inclined posts and tension wires hold the canvas rigidly in place.

Because the upper levels of buildings are physically removed from the humdrum business of everyday life, they make wonderful places to seek peace and tranquillity. In urban areas where gardens are rare luxuries, or even in rural areas where there is a desire to be separated from all things down-to-earth, the raised terrace or rooftop can be transformed into a magical, mystical place.

This fascination with height is nothing new. People have always inhabited rooftops – it is commonplace in warm countries to find rooftops used as courtyard gardens, dining areas or as places to sleep during the hottest summer nights. The habit of colonizing this space is now spreading further – even inner-city businesses are looking skyward and turning once shabby, grey asphalt roofs into simple but beautiful gardens for their staff. These are used for informal lunches and meetings and even as places to escape the distraction of the office to think in peace.

There is the same appeal in having a roof space at home. While many people like to add pavilions or other permanent structures, it is also worth considering the merit of informal, temporary structures to provide shade and a cool place to rest. These are usually a great deal cheaper than their permanent rivals and can be put in place during warm summer months, then dismantled and stored during the winter. Canvas sheeting is among the most versatile materials for this sort of

project. It can be simply strung across a space or stretched in a more sophisticated way across a frame to make a beautiful awning. Sail cloth is another popular option, being both lightweight and durable. Other materials include simple woven grass panels and screens – any material, in fact, which can withstand the summer weather. Think of the simple palm-frond thatch used in so many countries to provide dappled shade in which to retreat from the glare of the sun.

ABOVE **An intriguing sequence of horizontal blinds provides variable shade over this dining terrace. A solid roof would have made the space feel too thoroughly enclosed.**

case study – tea house retreat

As an addition to the traditional timber structure the architect-owner of this Japanese house wanted to create a series of new rooms that would delight and intrigue guests by offering them 'an experience of interesting space'. The new structures were also intended to provide a place for individuals to withdraw from the main body of the house and enjoy quiet thought. The spaces have an ethereal, and, for some, a spiritual quality.

The 'rooms' take their inspiration from the traditional tea house or *chashitsu*, which evolved as a miniature self-contained world for ritual and peace. The tea house has been built in Japan for many centuries and is believed to have reached a peak of perfection back in the 1500s. Traditionally, it is physically isolated from everyday life and inside, the space is clean, compact and orderly. The tea house was traditionally made with local materials put together with primitive simplicity. The space inside was deliberately small so that the occupants would be relieved of distraction and free to focus entirely on the tea ritual.

The architect set out to reinterpret these traditions centred on the ideas of separation and contemplation and the use of simple materials. Three new rooms – called tea houses – have been incorporated into the family town house, which has become an intriguing laboratory for new architectural ideas. The architect has explored the use and effects of different materials, aiming to restore the unity between house and nature that was lost in the modernization of Japanese houses in the '50s and '60s. The architect's fascination with light and shade, natural materials and the movement of air are all clearly evident in the new rooms. While many of the ideas and techniques are fresh, the spaces all obey – or owe some debt to – traditional Japanese design and its rigorous geometry.

The first tea house to be completed was called the Block Tea House and is actually built inside the house at ground-floor level. Its walls and floor are made using extremely smooth, polished concrete blocks, an exact 20 x 40 cm (8 x 16 in) each. The room measures 1.4 m (4½ ft) wide, 2.8 m (9 ft 4 in) long and 2 m (6½ ft) high. The restrained space is intended to create a solemnly spiritual world; a neutral corridor through which one passes to leave the world behind.

THE BRIEF: To create a series of rooms to give the home distinctive new types of space.
THE SOLUTION: Experimental use of diverse materials such as concrete, glass, steel, timber and canvas resulted in designs that reinvent the traditional Japanese tea house.

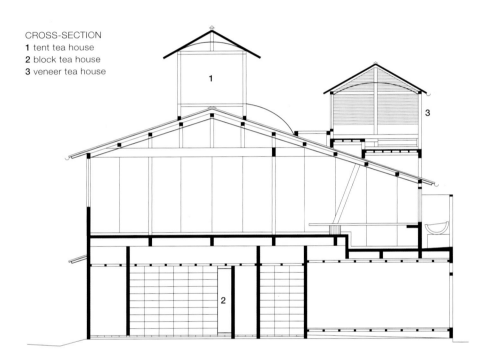

CROSS-SECTION
1 tent tea house
2 block tea house
3 veneer tea house

The remaining two tea houses are perched on the roof, providing an intriguing eyrie above the rooftops of Osaka. They share the qualities of simplicity and isolation but their very different materials result in distinctively different rooms.

The higher structure is called the Tent Tea House. It seems small and fragile, almost as if a gust of wind could carry it away. It has a canvas roof and walls that can be hoisted and lowered as required for protection against the weather or to provide open views; a strong metal frame provides the structure. Perhaps most surprising of all is the glass floor, which comes into its own in the evenings when the setting sun is reflected in the glass and casts a red glow.

The lower building is the Veneer Tea House, which was built using Japanese linden wood veneer panels and is based on the scale of the famous Myokian tea house. One wall is made from a bamboo screen, which allows in a dappled light. The room is reached by climbing a very steep stairway – often the traditional tea house was deliberately difficult to reach or had to be entered through a tiny door, so that visitors were conscious of entering somewhere special. Once inside, the aim of this Veneer Tea House is to create a space of such simplicity that there is a sense of endless depth and peace under the gently vaulted ceiling, and a sensual warmth in the timber walls.

ABOVE A view of the Veneer Tea House as seen from the Tent Tea House. The canvas wall of the Tent Tea House has been removed. The view from this angle does not take in the cityscape, but focuses on a much more confined area bounded by the walls of other buildings.

RIGHT The serene interior of the Veneer Tea House. Wood veneer was used for the floor, walls and ceiling. The curved ceiling is a clue to the perfect dimensions of the space – a 2.4m (7⅞ ft) diameter sphere would fit snugly into the interior, touching floor, walls and ceiling. At the far end is a bamboo screen which lets in soft filtered light and shadows.

going down

Some of the most inspiring design projects of recent years have been created from the least promising circumstances. And rarely is this more vividly demonstrated than in areas at the base of the home. Far from being fazed by the challenges of less-than-beautiful basements and cellars, architects and designers have produced stunning results. Whether it has been remodelling a ground-level basement space to introduce more light, excavating a cellar to make a habitable room or incorporating the precious extra space of an unused coal hole, the schemes demonstrate what is now possible. And as designs become more adventurous and building technology improves we see ever-more amazing schemes excavating whole suites of rooms under houses and even reaching out to tunnel under the garden.

There are variations in how people describe spaces at the foot of the home, but in this book a basement refers to the rooms at ground level or partially underground that are usually finished to a habitable level, a cellar refers to a storage room wholly underground, roughly finished and uninhabitable, and a coal hole is an exterior coal storage space at the front of the house and usually below road level.

3

LEFT **Unlocking the potential of basement areas has become a skill very much in demand from today's architects. These rooms can provide valuable additional living space.**

lighten up

To make any underground or lower-level space habitable concentrate on the quality and amount of natural light that will reach the interior. As we know from the rest of the house, the most enjoyable rooms are those bathed with sunlight, so architects and designers working on basement projects are continually devising ingenious ways of delivering as much light as possible.

Before any work starts, take a look at how the sunlight falls on this section of the building so that you can work out how to make the most of it. In the northern hemisphere, for example, a north-facing wall will never receive direct sunlight, but there may be ways to draw in plenty of ambient light. One

of the most widely used devices is the light well. As the name suggests this is a well of space where sunlight can fall. It is dug out, perhaps 1–2 m (3–6½ ft), from either the front or the back of the property and acts as a sun trap or sun scoop. To maximize the light it reflects into the interior, paint the sides of the well brilliant white.

In combination with the well, extra light can be drawn into the space through windows and glass doors. The larger the area of glass the more light will be let inside. But even the smallest windows – as tiny as 10 cm^2 (4 in^2) – can help to enliven an internal space. Take care to add security features to doors and windows

vulnerable to intruders. Think about piercing internal walls to make windows, too – this will not only provide intriguing views through the space, but will allow more light in. Large mirrors will also help to bounce light rays around the space.

Many basement-level extensions feature glass in the roof, either as large roof lights or as the entire covering. If this is an option, make sure there is easy access to the glass for cleaning. And finally, look out for opportunities to add glass panels in the floors above this space – a hole cut into a floor and replaced with a glass panel makes an unusual feature and will bring an interesting top light to rooms below.

case study – let there be light

The basement area of this building was typical of many nineteenth-century town houses – it was dark and carved into a warren of small rooms. However, the new owner wanted to incorporate the lower ground floor – formerly a self-contained apartment – into the rest of the house to provide a kitchen and informal, open-plan family living space.

The architect's task was tough – to stop the basement space feeling like a basement. The approach was to remove several internal walls, link the spaces and then perforate the external walls to allow more natural light to flood into the rooms. Work began by removing most of the internal walls, underpinning the remaining walls and fitting a series of steel frames (like goalposts) inside the structure to take the weight of the floors above. The continuous space now flows from a living area at the front of the house through to a central dining area and then kitchen at the rear. To one side is a lavatory and utility area. A new flight of stairs was added at the back of the space, reuniting the lower ground with the rest of the house above – previously there had only been external access from the front of the house.

The floor was dug out to provide additional ceiling height – around 10 cm (4 in) was gained. To protect the interior from the inevitable

THE BRIEF: To enlarge a self-contained basement flat and incorporate it with the rest of the house.
THE SOLUTION: The entire basement space was opened up, a kitchen extension added and more light was introduced through new windows, doors and glass floor panels.

problems with damp, a damp-proof course of a thick plastic membrane sheet was laid under the new concrete floor. A system of three renders provided damp protection for the walls. This type of render could not be tiled or painted with an oil-based paint as this would have interfered with its breathing properties and been a further cause of damp. Also, and for the same reasons, the surface could not be drilled, so where the client wanted to fit shelves, the wall was given an additional lining with plasterboard sitting in front of the render. Electrical wiring was held in plastic conduits sunk into the plaster.

Meanwhile, a kitchen was housed in a new back extension by enclosing an external courtyard. This was given an all-glass roof to draw in the maximum amount of sunlight. At the back of the kitchen a large sliding-glass door opens onto a small courtyard area.

BASEMENT FLOORPLAN
1 kitchen
2 dining
3 living
4 utility
5 lavatory

GROUND FLOORPLAN
6 glass roof over kitchen
7 glass roof over stairs
8 glass floor over dining

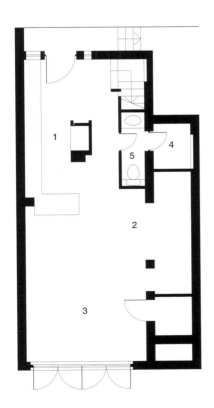

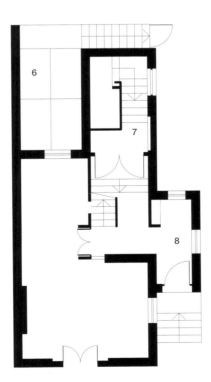

ABOVE An etched glass panel set into the roof is an ingenious way of drawing light down into a dingy interior. Even a fairly small panel can provide spirit-lifting volumes of sunlight. The etched lines cast a dappled light when the sun is very bright.

LEFT Throughout this project attention to detail and great use of natural and artificial light are a real feature. The window next to the dining area is just above the outside ground level, letting in valuable daylight. As well as being an interesting feature, a glass ceiling lets in light from the floor above.

Appealing details have been added into the design, including a large glass panel set into the hallway floor at ground level. This big rectangular area of glass draws a soft, diffused light down onto the dining table. The panel is not just an eye-catching feature: the quality of the space is hugely improved by introducing light right into the heart of the basement. The glass is finished with bands of etching for extra surface grip. To make sure this panel is safe and strong it is composed of two sheets of toughened glass – the top is 12 mm (½ in) thick and the one below is 19 mm (¾ in) thick. This 'sandwich' is devised to cope with the unlikely cracking of one of the glass sheets.

There is also subtle but interesting internal landscaping – the kitchen is given a degree of separation from the living area by being placed on a slightly raised platform. To boost light levels the sequence of new spaces is finished with white walls and a pale wood floor. This pale scheme helps to reflect light around the rooms. Another design device has been employed to enhance the sense of room height – walls are a sheer drop from floor to ceiling and have not been finished with skirting boards or decorative cornicing. This lack of visual distraction creates the illusion of taller rooms.

RIGHT **The basement sequence of spaces receives natural light from a variety of sources – from large French windows at the front, from the glass panel inset into the ceiling above the dining table and from the glass roof of the new kitchen extension.**

artificial lighting schemes

When it comes to designing a lighting scheme in a basement, and especially in underground rooms, the golden rule is to add more light fittings than you would in other parts of the house. This builds in plenty of opportunities for creating light settings for a range of moods and will also help to compensate for the reduced natural light at lower levels.

It is a good idea to start planning the scheme at the beginning of the building project, to make sure that the lighting is integrated with the rest of the design and not an awkward afterthought. Good planning can make a huge difference in helping a project run smoothly. Start to think early on about the position of switches and sockets and the best locations for wall, ceiling and even floor lights. For maximum control and flexibility add dimmer switches. In lower-ground projects electrical wiring is often run through the ceiling and in the upper parts of the room – this is to avoid any risk of wiring coming into contact with damp. You may also find that sockets are placed slightly higher up the walls than usual.

A basic scheme will begin with ceiling lights. Where the ceiling height is restricted it is advisable to use recessed fittings – a pendant light will become an annoying hazard. Of course, it depends on the shape of the room, but recessed lights usually look good and perform well when fitted around 50 cm (20 in) in from the wall and at perhaps 2 m (6½ ft) intervals

around the room. With the basics in place, think about adding additional lights to pick out features, such as eyeball spots to direct at a bookcase. Be creative with your scheme: ideas include twinkling low-voltage recessed lights in the shower, ankle-level lights recessed into the wall up a flight of stairs, or floor-recessed lights to give a wash of light up a wall. It is even possible to create fake 'windows' of light by back-lighting a window-sized glass panel set into the wall. The in-built scheme can be supplemented with table and floor lamps, so build those into the initial plan to ensure sockets are fitted in the right places.

Don't forget about exterior lighting. Here is a great opportunity to add interest outside at night by lighting up plants or other garden features. This will appear to extend the interior space by offering views beyond. Exterior lighting can provide extra background lighting for the interior on dull days or at night – by adding fittings into a light well, for example, the glow of light can be directed from the outside in.

ABOVE Where there is concern about poor light levels in a basement area, it is always a good idea to decorate in pale colours. A pale floor also helps to reflect light around the space. Ceiling recessed light fittings are advisable where ceiling heights are low.

LEFT Natural daylight does make its way into this elegant, basement bathroom. But for real drama and sparkle there is little to beat the low-voltage halogen lamp. These ceiling-recessed bathroom fittings are sealed units to protect against the damp atmosphere.

clever conversions

Transforming a storage cellar into a habitable space takes a considerable amount of imagination and skill. However, every pocket of space has potential. Unlike basements, the cellar is usually quite roughly finished, it may have a low ceiling height, be very small and may have no natural light at all.

There are two ways of approaching a transformation: the least expensive and least disruptive option is to make the most of the cellar pretty much as it is – is there enough room to make a utility space with washing machine and perhaps a freezer? Even by removing just a couple of these boxy items from the kitchen, you will benefit from more cooking space and will no longer have to listen to the washing machine in action. A larger cellar might be ideal as

a spare bathroom. If this is your chosen route, check that the area is fairly dry, not prone to flooding and that there is an electrical and water supply as well as drainage.

The second option is more complex but produces greater gains. This is to make the cellar into a habitable space, which is likely to involve full-scale building works. You may need to excavate to achieve comfortable floor-to-ceiling heights. Building regulations vary around the world, but a height of around 2 m (6½ ft) should be regarded as a minimum. You may also consider further excavation. Specialist companies have the expertise to dig out a small cellar to the size of a considerable room which may even have doors or a window to the garden.

ABOVE Although this is a small space, it has been beautifully finished and expertly planned to accommodate an entire kitchen. The attractive vaulted ceiling provides plenty of head height.

LEFT This cellar area has been transformed into a jewel of a room with wonderful mosaic finished walls, tiled floor and ceiling-recessed lighting. The exotic Eastern theme is picked up in the brass lanterns and the pretty carved screen across the window.

FAR LEFT With the minimum of effort this cellar space has been transformed into an additional grotto style of room. There's no natural light, but with thoughtful artificial lighting and a couple of comfortable sofas it takes on a new role as a hideaway or den.

converted coal holes

After reaching for the rafters, digging down into cellars, and pushing back every possible boundary wall, it is hard to imagine anywhere left for expanding our homes. And yet, amazingly, there still remains an unloved and largely under-used pocket of space lurking at the base of many older properties – the coal hole. With waterproofing, the addition of a window or roof light, ventilation and some creative planning, even this small space makes a useful addition. Recent conversions have included a galley kitchen, a utility area, a mini home gym and even a small office. Each case demonstrates that, as long as it is well planned, just a few square metres of extra floor space can make a huge difference to the home.

The coal hole was often built as a brick vault – the arched structure has great strength as well as visual appeal. Where the brickwork is still sound, it can be kept in place and used to house the conversion. The space can be linked to the rest of the house by adding a small lobby. It is entirely likely that you will need to excavate to gain sufficient ceiling height so, as with all underground structures, expect to carry out works to strengthen the foundations. However, where there are signs of structural deterioration like crumbling brick, it may be necessary to take more drastic action that, at its most extreme, could involve digging out the whole front-of-house area and starting from scratch. This, of course, is a more expensive option, but in the long run will add useful space.

ABOVE A compact kitchen with very narrow cupboards running down the lefthand wall, has been fitted into this converted coal hole. An area of the attractive brickwork has been left exposed as a reminder that this was once an outside space.

RIGHT Converted coal holes are put to a variety of uses. In this home there were two coal holes, one is now used to house the noisy washing machine and the other, shown here, has become a mini gym.

case study – bath spa in the cellar

THE BRIEF: To convert a disused cellar into a luxurious bathroom and sauna.

THE SOLUTION: Luxury is achieved by adding a ceiling of glass paving blocks, a huge bath and open-plan shower, underfloor heating, a sauna and a built-in music system.

This property was once a shop with living accommodation above. When it was taken over by its new owners – a couple with two young children – it was in very bad condition after years of neglect. As part of the renovation and modernization of the whole property, the cellar conversion presented a real challenge. It had no source of natural light, a low ceiling and no ventilation, but it did have the huge advantage of being extremely dry. At first the challenge to make a habitable space was too great and it seemed it could only provide useful storage room. However, the architect then hit on a scheme to introduce natural light. The shop front was pushed back approximately 1.5 m (5 ft) and in its place was set a room's width of glass paving blocks. The glass now provides beautiful light for the space, which has become the adult bathroom. The shop front faces south-east and so the sunlight is at its strongest all morning.

To make the most of this natural light, the bath and open-plan shower were fitted under the area of glass blocks. The walls were finished in soft grey tiles, which help reflect the natural light from above. This wet area is closed off from the rest of the bathroom by a screen of glass incorporating two simple, frameless glass doors.

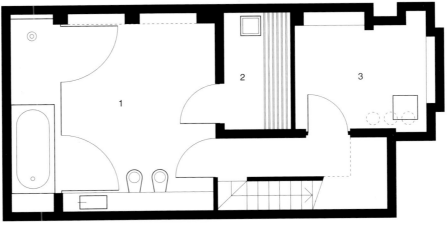

LEFT **The tiled area which contains the bath and open shower are separated from the rest of the bathroom suite by a screen of glass and a pair of frameless glass doors.**

ABOVE **The quality of the dappled light drawn into this bathroom is quite stunning. Appropriately enough, it almost has the feel of being under water.**

FLOORPLAN
1 bathroom
2 sauna
3 utility

As well as adding natural light, the works for this tranquil space included excavating to achieve a ceiling height of 2.1 m (7 ft), adding a damp-proof course, new concrete floor, underfloor heating and a finish of limestone paving. Because the brick walls were in good condition, they only required cleaning to restore them to their best. One wall features two beautifully built, recessed brick arches that form part of the original structure.

The lavatory and bidet were fitted to the wall at right angles to the bath. They sit below a long limestone counter with an in-built shallow rectangular basin. To create a sheer look, both were hung from the wall and all the plumbing pipes secreted behind panelling of Oregon pine. The same wood is also used to panel the outside of the sauna.

Drainage for the bathroom was easily achieved after a manhole was discovered in the floor of the small back room that houses the central heating boiler. Three mechanically powered air vents lead from the cellar to the outside to prevent any build up of damp.

Music adds the final touch of luxury. A quartet of speakers has been built into the ceiling, linking with the music system on the floor above. As in most bathrooms, the acoustics are excellent.

RIGHT **Three large light panels are set into the ceiling at pavement level. They are made from concrete into which is set a series of circular glass 'bricks'.**

digging deeper

The benefits of building underground are numerous. This increasingly popular building option opens up new posibilities for home owners. It creates the potential for space that is well insulated, able to maintain a steady room temperature and extremely energy efficient. The added advantage of building downwards is that it may provide a way of extending your living space in historic or protected areas where extensions may be restricted.

Some of the largest excavation projects have included sinking entire houses underground. However, to add more space to an existing property beyond the usual basement extension, a daring option is to dig under the garden. The process begins by stripping away the turf and any planting, then excavating a pit to the desired size. The hole is then lined with reinforced concrete and waterproofing material, a roof is added and the garden can be replaced over the top. To give an idea of scale, in one recent job some 300 tonnes of soil were removed to create a large new subterranean living room 79 m^2 (850 ft^2) in size.

Excavating can be expensive work, but it is possible to gauge whether it might be a good investment by breaking down the architect and builder's quotations into a price per square metre. Compare this with the value of your existing home per square metre or ask a local estate agent to estimate the value of the property with works completed.

ABOVE From the outside there are few clues about what lies beneath this gravel. This was exactly the effect desired by the local planning department, which was concerned about new building in this protected conservation area.

LEFT The underground space is quite beautiful and generously lit by the long central rooflight and even longer glass roof, to the left of the ceiling beam, which stretches the entire length of the room. Ceiling-recessed halogen light fittings add sparkle to the interior.

case study – from cellar to sunny playroom

THE BRIEF: **To create a children's play area and utility room.**
THE SOLUTION: **A dark under-hall cellar was extended sideways under the main living room. New windows introduced much-needed natural light and stairs were added to improve access.**

If a family still needs space when the attic has been converted and an extension has been built into the garden, moving house might appear to be the only option. However, increasing numbers of people are discovering the value of that extra space under their house. A children's playroom or family living room is one of the most popular uses for this new, lower-ground space.

An under-hall cellar already existed in this town house. This long, narrow strip of space, accessed by stairs under the main staircase, had its floor level excavated and lowered by more than a metre. For the new room alongside the existing cellar, digging started at the front of the house, creating a deep light well and then continued under the ground-floor living room towards the rear of the house. The excavations stopped before reaching the back wall, creating a large open-plan living space. Light enters through a large bay window built to match the existing window on the level above. Foundations were underpinned for extra support. Outside the window is a generous light well, painted brilliant white to reflect as much natural light as possible into the room.

The new space had to be fully damp-proofed using a system that incorporates pumps to remove any water that might collect.

One of the most appealing features of this space is the broad, open-tread, oak and steel stairway connecting the lower space with the living area and

ABOVE **A bespoke oak and steel stairway is fitted at the back of the newly excavated basement living space. Not only does this draw light down into the room, but it also means that parents can keep a watchful eye on children playing below.**

LEFT **The new play area is tailor-made for children with its recessed television, space enough for several children to play together and lots of storage space to tidy away toys at the end of the day.**

FAR LEFT **Natural daylight is drawn into the new basement bay window from the light well that has been excavated in the front garden. The white painted finish helps to reflect daylight indoors.**

ABOVE Along with a scaled-down play table and chairs, there is also a built-in desk with computer. This has been tucked away in a relatively quiet corner, away from the television, and is used for homework.

RIGHT The room is finished to high standards with a pale timber floor and good quality ceiling recessed lighting. Excellent design details include the wall recesses made for the television and video recorder, which protect this equipment from risk of accidental damage.

BASEMENT FLOORPLAN
1 new lightwell
2 play area
3 study recess
4 utility
5 lobby
6 store

BASEMENT CROSS-SECTION
7 new lightwell
8 play area
9 study recess
10 ground floor

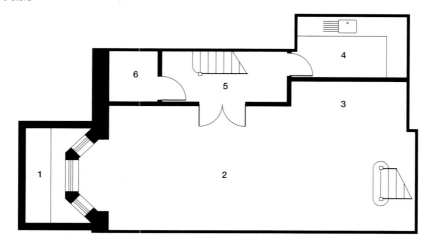

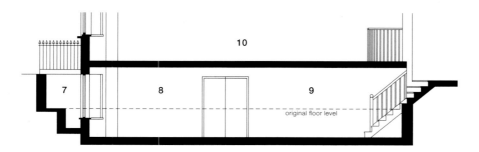

original floor level

kitchen above. As well as providing a stunning central staircase to connect the levels, the design also gives great views into the lower space so that adults can keep a watchful eye on children at play. As an added bonus it also lets natural light into the back of the room. Artificial lighting is provided by ceiling-recessed light fittings. There are also recessed fittings added to the walls of the exterior light well.

The finishes that were chosen make the most of the natural light, with white walls and a blonde wood floor. There is also lots of built-in storage space finished with flat-fronted, floor-to-

ceiling doors. Pale-coloured, sheer, reflective surfaces help to create an illusion of greater space than schemes incorporating rich colours or elaborate decoration.

In addition to this playroom, the design includes a generous utility room fitted with a washing machine and dryer and cupboards. This is an ideal extra space for a family, as it locates the noisy business of washing away from the living areas and frees up extra kitchen space. Here, a window was considered unnecessary, but to stop any build up of moisture, there is a mechanical extractor with exterior vent.

going out

For many homeowners, the garden extension is the easiest and most readily achievable way to add more space. For more than a century this has been achieved by fixing glass conservatories to the back or side of the house. However, in recent times, architects and designers have completely reinvented the garden extension and demonstrated their dazzling engineering skills by making beautiful and hard-working spaces. The most adventurous clients have found that their new extensions have provided them not only with a new room, but also a refreshing way of redesigning and enjoying their whole living space. In one project the client was so delighted with his sunny, light-filled, contemporary-style extension that he knocked down the rest of his house so that it could be rebuilt in the new style.

By building outwards, we have the opportunity to re-orient the home, blur the boundaries between inside and out and make the most of our garden spaces. Sometimes we may want to add a whole new annexe; in other cases a light-dappled terrace is all that is needed. In either case extending outwards can be one of the most rewarding adventures in creating a new space.

LEFT **Some of the most exciting ways of adding more space to the home have been built as garden extensions. Architects have shown that there are more imaginative ways to extend than by tacking on a conservatory.**

4

the new conservatory

No longer the outsider it once was, the conservatory is being reinvented as an integral part of everyday life. Of course, it is still possible to buy off-the-shelf designs that borrow from nineteenth-century conservatories and glass-house tradition, but for many people a bespoke contemporary extension is a more exciting and useful option.

The conservatory has evolved considerably since it was first created as a new incarnation of the orangerie and glass house, a place not just for the conservation of exotic plants, but also a room for relaxation. In its original form, the conservatory was a building composed mostly of glass held in a lattice framework. It was very clearly a transitional space, poised between house and garden, and plants remained a significant feature. Nowadays, the conservatory or glass extension is unlikely to act as a hot house; the emphasis is now much more on making a continuation of the interior. Its most popular uses are as a dining room or kitchen; a space for entertaining friends. As well as being a social space, we want the contemporary conservatory to be light-filled and sunny, perhaps almost completely blurring the boundaries between the house and garden. In many designs the extension leads directly onto an outside terrace – often the same flooring materials are used inside and out to make a visual link between the areas. This range of new uses has placed different demands on today's designers.

ABOVE **This striking, curved modern glass garden pavilion stretches out from the red brick house and reaches down into the garden. It provides a valuable extension to the home's kitchen and dining area and is linked to the garden by a series of cream stone terraces.**

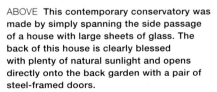

ABOVE **This contemporary conservatory was made by simply spanning the side passage of a house with large sheets of glass. The back of this house is clearly blessed with plenty of natural sunlight and opens directly onto the back garden with a pair of steel-framed doors.**

ABOVE RIGHT **This unusual double-storey conservatory extension manages to scoop up plenty of natural light for the interior through its attractive peeled-back roof. In place of roof tiles, a simple skirt of glass panels is wrapped around the curved end of the structure.**

The position of the extension in relation to the sun is crucial. In the northern hemisphere, for example, a conservatory or all-glass extension facing due south will almost certainly become unbearably hot in the summer, so it may be advisable to build a solid roof which affords some protection from the sun. It is also worth considering whether the space will be used all through the winter. If so the luxury of including underfloor heating is well worth exploring.

Although these extensions feel very much like garden buildings, you may need planning permission for their construction. There is an erroneous prevailing belief that glass-roof structures don't require planning permission – a cause of much contention – but regardless of the materials used it is advisable to check before you start the project.

all clear: glass extensions

ABOVE **To extend this brick-built town house, the architect added a two-storey glass conservatory extension. The design could have been a pastiche of the main house, but instead the owners opted for visual excitement and an uncompromising, contemporary addition.**

When building an extension largely of glass, the type of glass you use will be a major consideration. Manufacturing technology has made significant progress in recent decades, making it possible to make sheets of glass the size of walls, and high-performance glass that helps control temperature and glare. The choice of materials may be confusing, but the following are the main options. The types of glass you are most likely to encounter are toughened or laminated. Toughened

(or tempered) glass is strengthened by re-heating the sheet to just below its melting point and then suddenly cooling it. It is five times stronger than standard glass and when shattered, it breaks into small pieces. In many countries it is required as safety glazing in patio doors, entrance doors and other vulnerable locations. One drawback is that it cannot be re-cut after tempering. Laminated glass is a sandwich of two or more sheets with an inner layer of transparent plastic.

When broken the glass fragments stick to the plastic layer. It is used as safety glass and for sound insulation.

The other types of glass you will encounter are 'low-e' and tinted or solar-reflective glass. Glass-coating technology has been developed to control the sunlight and heat that pass through the glass. 'Low-e' or low-emission coating is a microscopically thin, virtually invisible, metal or metallic oxide layer fixed to the glass. It reduces the U-factor – the heat loss or gain through the glass. Glass described as 'high solar gain, low-e' admits heat and light and keeps the heat inside – ideal for a room without direct sunlight. Another version is 'low solar gain, low-e', which lets light in but reduces the amount of heat that penetrates the glass – perfect for rooms in the full heat of the sun. Glass with a tinted or solar-reflective finish has a film on the glass surface to reduce the light and heat of the sun – just like sunglasses.

ABOVE **A highly unusual glass extension was added to this converted industrial building. In several places around the exterior, a glass extension was hooked onto the outside.**

LEFT **This is an exquisitely designed and superbly crafted glass extension to a nineteenth-century town house. The quality of the finishes is of the very highest order and the architect has even designed much of the furniture.**

case study – extension cube

This extension was designed to fit exactly within the size limits allowed without the time-consuming business of applying for planning permission. In this particular area the maximum size of 'permitted development' is 50 m³ (65 cubic yards). Any larger, and it could have taken up to six months for the application to be processed. So the extension was conceived as a perfect minimal wrapper for the maximum space – 3.85 m long, 3.7 m wide and 3.5 m high (12 ft 8in long, 12 ft wide and 11½ ft high).

The new structure was added at the back of the house as an extension to the dining room. To ensure the spaces flow together, the floor level of the new cube is the same as the dining room. Since the garden is slightly lower, the cube was raised on steel legs encased in concrete.

Although the extension appears to be built of wood, the frame is actually constructed of steel. One of the early plans was to prefabricate the whole addition off site, and then hoist it over the roof and into position with a crane. However, shortage of workshop space made that impossible. In the end, the whole structure was brought through the house in sections – the windows are the maximum size possible to fit through the front door. With the frame in place, the party wall was finished with zinc on the outside and plaster on the inside, with the remaining two walls in glass. Insulation was a prime concern and so the solid wall, roof and floor are packed with insulating

FLOORPLAN

1 lavatory   6 dining
2 hall   7 pottery
3 living   8 extension
4 play room   9 deck
5 kitchen

ABOVE The view looking from the house through the cube to the garden. The doors are finished in white to blend with the walls.

LEFT With both doors open there is a clear sense of how the spaces flow unhindered from the kitchen to the lawn.

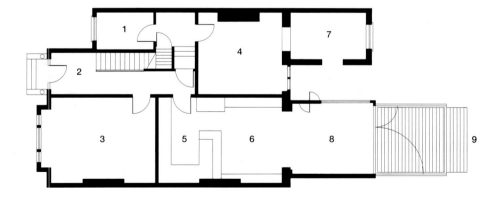

THE BRIEF: Construct a contemporary space to enjoy views of the garden whatever the weather.

THE SOLUTION: A perfect cube of glass, steel and wood that links house and garden.

material. The double-glazing is made with toughened glass on the outside and is laminated on the inside.

Although it looks simple, the cube is exquisitely built and finished; the cedar cladding is particularly impressive and has been fitted from the inside of the frame so that there are no screws visible on the outside. Even the doors are made with a metal frame and a cedar finish. Cedar is also used for the frame wrapped round the metal balustrading.

Two doors make up the wall that opens onto the garden – one is of normal width and the other is an extra-wide panel. Because of the weight of the larger door, it is hung on special hinges and swings open with the help of a roller wheel on its leading edge. This sits in a stainless steel arc of track embedded in the cedar deck. The larger door is bolted in place most of the time, while the smaller one is used for everyday access. However, on warm days, both can be fully opened and used as screens to the deck, which extends beyond the cube. The deck is exactly the same size as the cube floor, so with both doors open the floor area is doubled.

The hidden guttering is another great detail – pipes would have ruined the elegance of the design. The roof is a shallow pyramid shape and the guttering is fitted around its edges behind the cedar frame. The rainwater then flows back towards the house and runs away through a drain pipe fitted in a recess.

LEFT The design of the cube draws on a very different style to the main home, yet the extension does not seem out of place. The regularity of the cube echoes the square window panes of the house and the colour of the wood is sympathetic to the brickwork.

extended highlights

There are occasions when something more substantial than a conservatory is required. Designs which incorporate a greater expanse of solid wall than glass can become invaluable and even seamless additions to the living space.

In planning such an extension, first consider what sort of new space would be most useful – do you need an additional bedroom or bathroom, or would it be better to open up the ground floor area? This should help you to decide whether you need a one or two storey extension.

It is also worth thinking about the balance and position and flow of rooms. For example if your home has four bedrooms, one bathroom and a

small living space, then clearly extra living space would be welcome. But you might also try to incorporate an additional bathroom since this will help alleviate pressure during the morning and night-time bathing rush hours. An extra bathroom will add to your home's value too – a wise investment.

Building on a new extension also opens up the possibility of reshaping or reordering the internal spaces and improving the flow of rooms. For example, in most homes the hub of activity is centred on the kitchen, and, as we have seen in recent years, the trend has been to link that space with the outdoors whether it is a garden or even a small courtyard. As a result, the traditional layout in homes designed before the 1950s needs to be refocused with the emphasis on cooking and dining being opened up and linked with the garden. The surge of interest in making the garden an extra 'room' also means that good access from the new extension is vital – big sliding or folding doors are a good idea, and so too are design details such as making the floor level match that of the garden or courtyard.

Think about security too – large expanses of glass can be vulnerable to burglars. Consider using toughened glass, and check that your locks are efficient. If the new doors are very vulnerable, take advice from security specialists who may suggest incorporating a protective metal screen which can be drawn across the opening when you are away.

LEFT This is an unusual extension for such a traditional house. But the zinc-grey curved roof is a close colour match to the house's grey roof tiles and the two sit well together.

ABOVE The large open-plan space makes a stylish living area. The link with the garden is seamless and is helped by the fact that the inside and outside floors are the same level.

INSET The same extension as above, but viewed from the outside. The huge glass windows allow the eye to roam to the end of the kitchen and give an impression of space.

into the woods

Building with wood is enjoying a welcome renaissance, and not just where it might be expected in rural homes – it is also being used in urban settings in exciting and intriguing ways.

Because of its ready availability, timber was one of the earliest building materials and during the Middle Ages it became the staple for just about every dwelling. However, the Industrial Revolution brought the mass production of other building materials – brick, in particular. In many areas it replaced wood as a more durable and less flammable product.

The current renewed popularity of building with wood is driven by a number of factors. The green lobby sings its praises both as a renewable building material and one which is environmentally friendly in its production, particularly when compared with options like brick, which requires a huge amount of energy to manufacture. This enthusiasm has had a knock-on effect, with many architects and designers being inspired to use the material in new ways and to experiment with combining the latest timber construction technologies with contemporary design. There has also been considerable research into the strength and durability of timber that demonstrates, for example, that in many projects oak beams can perform just as well as steel in supporting massive weights, but also that many hardwoods offer surprisingly high levels of fire resistance. Some timbers are incredibly resistant to the extremes of weather and are so hardwearing that they have a life expectancy running into many decades – the hardwood iroko, for example, if used as an exterior cladding, can be expected to look good for at least 50 years. In addition to this, homeowners have rediscovered their affection for a material which is natural, beautiful, has good green credentials, is easy to work with and can be cheaper than building with other materials.

The use of wood in home extensions is particularly appropriate – at one extreme it was a feature of many of the grand conservatories of the nineteenth and early twentieth centuries, at the other, it can be as simple and familiar as the garden shed. Timber structures are extremely evocative – many of us have fond memories of wooden beach huts, summer houses, log cabins, tree houses and the hand-made den at the bottom of the garden.

However, as with all products, there are inevitably a few drawbacks. For example, many people assume that because wood is a natural material it must also be healthy. This is not always the case, however, as the natural and strong-smelling aromatic terpenes in pinewood resin can cause some people to suffer an allergic reaction when they breathe it in. Also, there continue to be problems with assurances that wood is produced in the most sustainable way. A number of

environmental pressure groups urge consumers to avoid buying mahogany because much of the Brazilian product is known to be cut illegally and is damaging the rainforests.

If you are considering using wood and want to be sure that it is sustainably produced, use one of the growing numbers of eco builders' merchants or a timber merchant that can guarantee the source. You could also consider using the recycled timber available from architectural salvage yards.

ABOVE The timber and glass extension on stilts makes a wonderful lookout post for this countryside home. It is in fact used as a study. The family house has been extended and remodelled a number of times, and with each project is opened up and made yet lighter inside. Built with a steel frame, clad in iroko and standing on oak posts, the new study also doubles as a porch.

LEFT Long-lasting and sustainably farmed iroko hardwood is the main material used in the cladding and decking of this new extension. The use of the same wood for walls and decking creates a pleasing visual effect. The doors to the deck slide back to give great garden views and enable adults to keep an eye on children at play.

everybody needs good neighbours

Neighbours often receive very bad press. Newspapers and television programmes take great delight in exposing neighbourly feuds, but occasionally the stereotype is shattered and faith is restored in humankind. Of course, neighbours have traditionally united in adversity to fight off unwanted developments, new roads and restrictive parking regulations, but there are occasions when neighbours joining forces have produced unique results. In many towns and cities groups of neighbours have taken down their fences so that their children can play safely in communal back gardens; others save money and hassle by booking decorators to paint a row of houses.

Occasionally, households cement relations and cut costs by joining forces on building projects. Working together on new extensions makes perfect sense. Not only is it financially advantageous to share an architect for one set of plans, but it also means that materials can be bought in bulk and that a builder can be employed to see the joint project through to the end. It also means just one period of disruption for the building works. A collaborative effort can also ensure that both parties are entirely happy with the designs, which ensures a swift path through the process of applying for and being granted planning permission. Recent joint projects have demonstrated that it is possible to save as much as one-third of the cost of going it alone.

ABOVE Each half of this jointly built kitchen extension has been finished according to the owner's design and taste. This half is painted white and has blonde wood fitted wall and base units.

LEFT The other kitchen is painted a rich cobalt blue and is fitted only with base units.

FAR LEFT Seen from the outside, it is clear that this joint project was built as a single job. There is a shared central wall and roof and the garden doors were made in similar designs with the same materials. By joining forces these neighbours calculate that they have saved almost one third of the cost of building two separate extensions.

joined-up thinking

If you have the opportunity of teaming up with neighbours to add more space to your homes, it can be a great way of building solid relationships. There are countless occasions when teamwork can pay off – the classic back extension is clearly a great idea, but one- and two-storey extensions work equally well. Other ideas include adding twin front porches, new dormer windows that run across two roofs or even a whole extra storey to each of a pair of houses. The most unusual example by far is in a block of apartments where neighbours united to add a large balcony to each floor.

The key to a successful joint project is to ensure good communication right from the beginning and to check that

all parties concerned want to achieve the same or very similar results. All too often, neighbours first learn about a proposed building project when the planning notice is pinned up outside or in the local paper. The natural response is to be defensive. It is far better to discuss plans together from the start.

In a collaborative project the first step is to discuss your ideas, make sketches showing how the plan might work and find out if the neighbour is interested in joining you. If you need an architect, draw up a shortlist of candidates and arrange meetings together. The same goes for builders. Every design detail must be considered and agreed. There are sure to be some differences of opinion, so keep an open mind – your neighbour

may have suggestions that improve the original idea and produce a more interesting result. With the brief established, ask your architect to draw up a written agreement on the works being undertaken.

Because building works of any sort are disruptive, they are almost inevitably going to be stressful, so make sure you can both cope with the mess. It is also crucially important to settle on a budget and to make sure you both have the funds available. Finally, be well organized and keep records and receipts of every transaction so that everyone knows how their money is being spent. Once the ground rules have been established, a collaborative venture can be very rewarding.

ABOVE Three neighbours in this converted industrial building had all been thinking about adding some sort of terrace or balcony to their apartments. When they joined forces they were able to afford this triple deck extension giving each apartment an additional 9 x 3m (29½ x 9¾ft) outside area. The top sun deck, shown here, has a retractable canvas roof for protection against strong sunshine.

LEFT AND INSET The multi-storey, lightweight steel extension appears to be hung on the outside of the building – however it is also supported on poles from the ground. Each deck is finished with glass panels as side screens and balustrading.

open to the elements

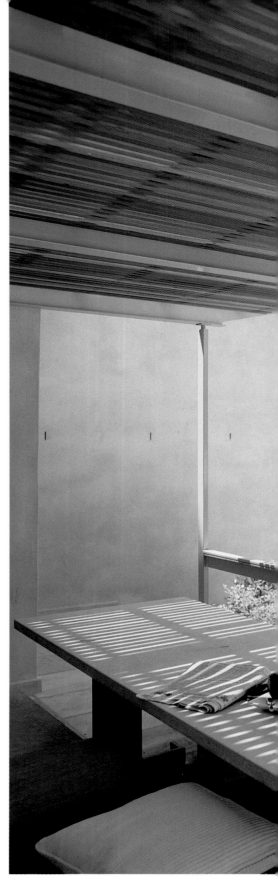

ABOVE There could hardly be a more dramatic backdrop for dining than this stunning landscape. To make the most of the views, this luxurious terrace has been turned into an outdoor dining room. The impressive design incorporates monumental stone pillars and a slatted timber roof, there is also a large stone serving bench and a built-in barbecue.

RIGHT Altogether more informal in tone than the terrace shown above, this simple dining area frames great views and, with its slatted timber roof, gives protection from the fierce sun.

If you'd like to extend your home, but not at the expense of precious outdoor space, a structure that is partly open to the elements could be the answer.

Architects are constantly looking at ways to redefine the relationship between indoor and outdoor spaces; many new design projects look to exploit that transitional area between the exterior and interior. In most cases, glass in the form of huge windows or sliding and folding doors is used to provide the thin barrier of protection from the elements. However, in other homes, designers have turned to the traditional porch or veranda as a way of making space that is an outdoor extension of the living area but which

is sheltered from the extremes of weather. In Hindi the word *veranda* translates as an open deck or platform that sits alongside the house, but interpretations of the idea vary widely from a small open balcony to a gallery the size of a room. Most are finished with a light roof held on post supports.

For such an informal space, simplicity is often the key. Structures can be as basic as a canvas awning drawn from the house and over a portion of the garden. At the other end of the scale, they may involve a more permanent arrangement with a solid floor – perhaps in stone or timber – and then timber, brick or masonry supports and a roof.

The choice of materials is extremely important as it will set the mood of the new structure – canvas and wood are clearly reminiscent of temporary shelters such as tents and marquees and are therefore great for marking out spaces for relaxing. Here you can sink into piles of cushions, rest on a rug and snooze in the shade. However, an area finished in marble, fine ceramics and hardwoods is clearly a more serious investment of time, effort and money and therefore becomes a place for entertaining and more permanent furnishings. Here you might include a wood or metal dining table, a built-in barbecue or luxuries like a fridge and electric lighting. Whichever style of addition is most appropriate, the most enjoyable of these spaces will ideally frame a view and make a new outside 'room' in the garden.

case study – curvaceous kitchen

This sleek Modernist home was built back in the late 1950s as a classic flat-roof villa, but during the intervening half century it has been substantially altered and extended. When the new owners wanted to expand the place as a family home the choice was either to try to rediscover and recreate the original building or to extend in a twenty-first-century style. Since the original had been so extensively altered, the decision was taken to make bold new additions, including a bedroom suite and kitchen.

The architect's kitchen design was conceived as a distinctive, expressive gesture – a big wave of timber that curls upwards from the exterior deck and through the kitchen floor. It then curves at the wall, stretches up over the ceiling and finally bursts outside to provide shelter for the deck.

THE BRIEF: **Build a new kitchen as part of the refurbishment and extension of a 1950s house.**

THE SOLUTION: **A highly unusual kitchen extension in bold contrast to the original style.**

LEFT Looking along the sheer stainless steel worktop towards the back of the kitchen, the unusual shape of the space tapers to a narrow wood-clad wall.

ABOVE The kitchen units are clad with a veneer that uses pine that has been stained and finished to give the appearance of a rich hardwood.

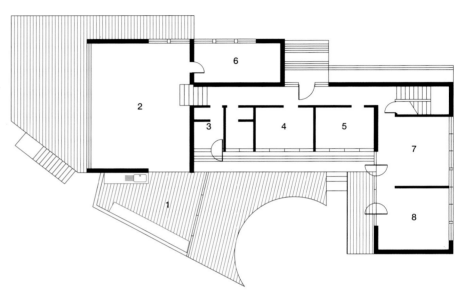

GROUND FLOORPLAN

1 kitchen	**5** bedroom 2
2 living	**6** cellar
3 laundry	**7** bedroom 3
4 bedroom 1	**8** bedroom 4

The contemporary style kitchen fits into a small wedge-shaped piece of land beside the living area. The architect describes it as being 'almost like a small caravan that has been parked alongside the main house'. It is built very simply with a steel frame and corrugated metal roof. The front wall is clad entirely in glass and opens onto the timber deck and grass courtyard. Inside, the space is divided between the cooking wall, which has excellent views, and the sheer-fronted storage wall with plenty of room for a dining table and chairs in between. The predominant materials are timber and metal – the floor and ceiling being polished with tung oil. The worktop is a continuous run of stainless steel.

UPPER FLOORPLAN
9 deck
10 study
11 bathroom
12 master bedroom

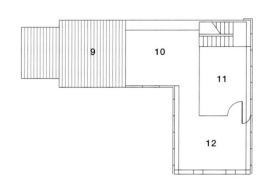

TOP LEFT The view from the new roof terrace is framed by this 'window' in the wall, which looks down across the front of the kitchen to the landscape and eucalyptus trees and camellias beyond. The wooden screen affords privacy from passers-by below, making a perfect rooftop retreat.

RIGHT The dramatically curved shape of the kitchen extension acts as a scoop for the fantastic views and abundance of natural sunlight. The front wall of the kitchen is finished in glass panels with large glass doors that open onto the sheltered wooden dining terrace.

inside out

ABOVE **This deck is almost as thoroughly furnished as any room inside the house. There is an upholstered sofa and chairs, coffee table and big piles of cushions. The area is fringed with massive potted plants. The owners clearly intend to spend as much time as possible out here enjoying the summer weather.**

RIGHT **This deck area is a minimal affair. It is accessed by sliding back the huge glass-panel doors and is kept free of plants and furniture, but on warm days and evenings it becomes the ideal place to relocate the dining table outside.**

The deck has become the new back yard. After decades of popularity in North America, this outside platform has now started to gain fans all round the world. The great appeal of the deck is that it provides a simple extension to the living space – here the doors can be thrown open and the home immediately rolls out into the garden. It is slightly more formal (and more practical) than a lawn, and even though there are neither walls nor roof, it does have a sense of structure and the feeling of a room. Traditional timber decking is particularly appealing because of its warmth, natural texture and pattern. For anyone who has spent time on boats, a warm, sunny deck will always be reminiscent of the very best summer days and evenings.

It is an important part of the planning process to decide how the new deck will be used – those close to the house are most often built as an exterior dining and living area. Where space is restricted, you may be limited to a small sundeck, but where there is plenty of room, you could build in a barbecue or hot tub. Remember that water is incredibly heavy – some 1 tonne per cubic metre (64 lb per cubic foot) – so a tub will need plenty of structural support. Decking can be left entirely unadorned, providing a 'bridge' between inside and the garden, or it can be furnished and decorated with plants much like a traditional terrace or patio. However, getting the size right is vital to making sure this will be a handsome and useful new space – the most common mistake is to overestimate the floor area. If it is too large it will be out of proportion with the scale of the house.

The first step in planning is to mark out the proposed deck area with posts and string. It is a good idea to place a table and chairs inside the string to gain a sense of the proportions. If the space is to be used as a dining area, make sure there is room to move the chairs around and to sit comfortably at the table without being perched on the deck edge.

While marking out the space, it is also important to take into account fixtures such as manhole covers, drain pipes, boiler vents, phone lines and trees. For example, if the deck is fitted over a manhole cover, it may be necessary to build in an access hatch for maintenance. When it comes to trees, make sure a sizeable hole is left for the trunk. Many decking companies provide collars to fit round trees so there is no danger of tripping or twisting your ankle in the holes. Think carefully about placing decking near trees because you will inevitably have to clear up when the leaves fall – dripping sap and leaf-mould will leave unsightly stains.

Another important step is to chart the sun's path – a deck without sun can be gloomy, while a deck with full sun may need some shady shelter incorporated into the design. Finally, before any building starts, check to see whether the local authority requires formal planning permission.

rooms without walls

When decking moves further into the garden there are new considerations. The further from the house, the more likely this will be an informal space more closely integrated with the garden and general landscape. Do you intend to use it as an outside 'room', a hideaway sundeck, a raised walkway or a lookout post? Whichever you choose, it remains a good idea to stake out the proposed area with string to get a sense of its size. Don't feel constrained to use a regular square or rectangular shape. This might be a great opportunity to introduce irregular decking, perhaps fitting it around shrubs, a pond or plant beds. Decking also looks stylish when used in terraces on sloping sites – the layers of timber can provide an

exciting series of platforms where it would be impossible to maintain a lawn. Think about safety features – raised platforms or flights of steps will usually require some form of handrail.

Visit a number of decking suppliers to see what is available. Some may offer off-the-shelf circular decks, panels of timber that can be assembled into interesting shapes or ready-made flights of stairs. This is also the time to explore how the deck will be assembled and fixed in place. Most systems are based on buried concrete footings onto which the posts and then beams and joists of the structure are fixed. The deck boarding sits on top of this structure and holds it all in place. If the proposed site is a particularly tricky

terrain, perhaps very rocky, it is a good idea to take a few photographs to show your decking supplier to make sure your plans can be carried out.

There are several types of decking material – the traditional cedar and redwood timbers have been joined by an array of composite materials and plastics. Man-made materials may seem an attractive option being low maintenance or maintenance free, but there are drawbacks. Some plastics can be difficult to install and the man-made materials have been known to sag slightly when exposed to intense heat from the sun. Timbers are easy to handle but will eventually be subject to ageing and rotting and do require some maintenance to extend their life.

ABOVE This high-level deck reaches out into the landscape and appears to stretch into infinity. It is pierced in one area to let light fall into the garden below. Safety railing is an absolute necessity.

RIGHT Timber decking can be put to a multitude of uses, in this garden it begins as a raised deck close to the house and then stretches deep into the garden to make a zig-zag pathway through the planting scheme.

LEFT This very neat and precise scheme features unusual narrow slatted timber for decking. The dining area is set away from the house in a spot that enjoys good sunshine.

the room beyond

There is something unmistakably handsome, monumental and noble about stone. Often used in the construction of our most prestigious buildings, it has powerful connotations, evoking durability and timelessness. Stone is also expensive and so when used in a domestic setting, and as a terrace, is very grand.

The range of stones on offer is enormous and many specialists have access to materials from all round the world. The wide colour spectrum and choice of texture makes it possible to select anything from rich jet-black slates or stippled granite to marble shot through with vivid colours or even the palest, creamiest limestone. The market is also well provided with composite materials such as paving slabs made of stone chips or glass set in concrete, or simply concrete used alone in slabs or as a poured material. Of course, budget will be a major factor in helping to decide which finish to choose, but there are other elements to think about too. Does the stone work well with the other materials used in the home? Does it match or provide an interesting contrast? Does it look comfortable with the surrounding garden and landscape? Think about the size and shape of slabs available – an ordinary stone tile, perhaps 30 cm^2 (12 in^2) square, will have much less visual impact than the same stone in really huge slabs. Rectangular shapes might look good, too. Your stone supplier should know which stones and quarries are able to provide paving in interesting shapes made to order.

The key to creating a beautiful, stone-lined terrace is in making sure the preparatory work is of an extremely high quality. The base must be solid, level and well drained. Unless you have experience in this area, this really is a job for a professional. Some of the most stunning effects can be achieved when the same material is used inside and out and the flooring is laid as a seamless surface. When the terrace doors are open there is a natural flow between the interior and exterior.

The choice of stone should be based on a mixture of aesthetics and practicality. If you opt for a pale, smooth-faced limestone and you want it to stay that way, it is likely to require regular maintenance. Any build up of fallen leaves, tree sap or moss should be removed immediately and the surface may need regular washing with a gentle cleaning agent. Limestone requires an alkaline cleaner – anything acidic will eat away at the surface. It may also be a good idea to keep the surface free of permanent fixtures such as pots or garden furniture because these, too, are likely to stain the stone. However, if you are happy for the new stone terrace to take on a patina of age through exposure to the weather, then a material such as York stone may be more appealing. In all cases take advice from the stone supplier about which cleaning materials are recommended and whether a sealant is required.

ABOVE This pale limestone flooring flows almost seamlessly between indoors and out. This continuous surface helps to draw the eye to the garden beyond. The trio of red cylindrical planters is an eye-catching focal point of the view from inside.

LEFT A limited palette of materials helps to enhance the sense of space in any room and works particularly well in this dining terrace. The purity and serenity of the space requires regular maintenance to ensure there is no build up of leaves or other garden matter that might litter the area.

case study – glass double act

The design for this new extension is incredibly hard working. It not only provides views of the garden, and a link between indoors and out, but it also draws vast amounts of light into the newly remodelled interior and creates a stunning first-floor balcony.

As with many older homes the original basement was divided into a number of small rooms. Not surprisingly, the new owner wanted to open up the whole garden level to make a new kitchen and dining room as well as to provide access to the outdoors. The architect describes this process as 'paring away the old' and 'airing' the house. The back wall was removed and the new extension was pushed out into the garden. Where there had been a small lightwell, the architect dug out a large terrace area with steps leading up to the main garden level.

The frame of the new extension is delicate and made of slender posts of galvanized steel. At ground level it features two large glass doors that can be thrown wide open to make the most of the garden views. The roof is made from one huge, continuous slab of glass measuring 2.4 m (8 ft) long and 1.3 m (4 ft 4 in) wide. It is constructed from two sheets of toughened glass 25 mm (1 in) and 15 mm (½ in) thick, which have been laminated together. The uppermost

THE BRIEF: To open up a dark basement and link the new space to the garden.

THE SOLUTION: Remove the internal walls and add a new glass extension that can also double as a balcony.

LEFT Looking through the glass-floored balcony and into the extension below. The irregular pattern of stripes casts intriguing shadows below.

ABOVE A view of the garden looking through the new extension with the glass balcony floor now doubling as a ceiling. The slender-framed doors open onto the new terrace.

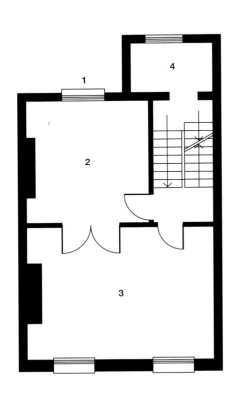

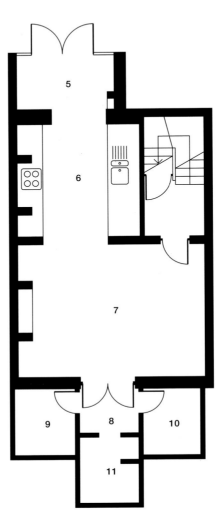

GROUND FLOORPLAN
1 balcony
2 library
3 living
4 extension

BASEMENT FLOORPLAN
5 conservatory
6 kitchen
7 dining
8 patio
9 laundry
10 wine cellar
11 central cellar

RIGHT **This picture clearly shows the lovely dappled shade produced by the etched glass roof. The line pattern is picked up again on the glass-fronted kitchen wall cupboards. The remodelled and simplified basement space now contains a kitchen and dining room.**

FAR RIGHT **Although the architect could have dispensed with much of the buildings old structure, including this section of wall, the decision was made to keep fragments of the original old walls to act as a visual reminder of how the house had been laid out. The new floor is made from a dark grey poured concrete.**

surface, which is the balcony to the formal living room above, was given an unusual acid-etched pattern of irregular stripes. This makes a non-slip surface for anyone standing on the balcony, but also casts a lovely dappled pattern of shade in the rooms below.

The interior spaces leading to the new extension have been opened up to make a contemporary-style kitchen and dining area. Interestingly, instead of removing the old walls altogether, the architect decided to cut large openings and leave some of the wall edge in place as a reminder of the original early nineteenth-century design. All new additions are very

clearly defined – instead of trying to imitate the past, the architect wanted to make it very clear what was new and what was old. A new floor was created with poured dark-grey concrete; this was laid at the same level as the York stone paving of the new terrace. The walls of the new area were left as plain render.

The unmistakable highlight of the new design is the glass roof/balcony. The rhythmic pattern of the irregular etched stripes has been picked up and echoed in the metal balustrade and this, too, helps to create the interesting pattern of shadows in the space below.

far out

Everybody needs a place to dream, a place to relax and a place to escape to from time to time. The space we make outside, away from the home, becomes important as an oasis of calm in our busy lives and can be a place of pure fantasy.

This urge to create another world is nothing new – humans have always sought to create different types of environments for different occasions and where there is the luxury of space, time and money, the garden has played host to the most imaginative, even fantastical structures. However, what was once the preserve of the rich has now become a fascination for growing numbers of us.

Where people in the past built follies and temples in the grounds of their large estates, we may now build a summer house, an office in the garden or perhaps a retreat in the shape of a tent or even a Mongolian yurt. Even the humble garden shed has its place in providing tranquillity and distance from everyday pressures. Whatever type of project we choose, the aim is to make it inspiring, beautiful, natural and uplifting to the spirits.

LEFT **Who could resist the idea of basking in the evening sun in this faraway place? The idyllic retreat needs to be separated from the pressures of everyday life.**

summer houses

The summer house has enjoyed a long history and possibly reached its apogee at the end of the nineteenth century in northern Europe when, in the grounds of grand houses, it provided welcome shade on hot days and the perfect setting for afternoon tea after a stroll. Rather like the conservatory, this appealing building has an air of gentility about it.

Some of the grandest garden structures were built as miniature temples, scaled-down houses, shell grottoes, man-made caves or even exotic follies, and were generally built using brick or stone. Today these are rarely commissioned and most new garden building tends to be rather more modest.

The summer house now comes in many guises – there remains the traditional-style pavilion, usually a timber-framed structure with generous windows, but there are also plenty of modern interpretations of the same theme. On a small scale, a summer house can look like a diminutive chalet, providing indoor shelter and perhaps a deck or veranda. Some of the cleverest designs even allow the building to rotate so that the occupants can choose to sit in full sun or shade as the sun follows its path across the sky. Sometimes these designs are as simple as a garden shed, but equally they can be as elaborate and exotic as the imagination will allow.

On a large scale, the summer house can be placed a long way from the main house and used for sleeping out on hot nights and for guest accommodation. In some countries, those in Scandinavia for example, the summer house is often a rural retreat, a second home located in a forest or at the beach and used for weekend escapes.

The essential character of the summer house is based on its simplicity and its relationship to nature, particularly the sun. This outdoor room offers shade when it gets too hot and a resting place in which to enjoy the fresh air and garden or landscape. In most cases wood and glass are the key materials, but the structure doesn't need to be built with the same level of finish found in a house. Simplicity and natural materials set the tone, but it is also important to incorporate an element of fantasy in the design and decoration to create an ideal hideaway, picnic spot, quiet retreat or somewhere to stretch out in the sun.

As ever there are practical considerations – even in remote rural locations you may still require planning permission for a summer house. And if the plan is to spend a lot of time there, it could be worth adding plumbing and a source of electricity. Don't assume that an off-the-shelf design will be cheaper than commissioning an architect – you may discover that it is possible to build a bespoke design at a very competitive rate.

ABOVE **This jaunty and rather quirky design makes a great summer house. Inside there is shelter from heat or cold and yet has enough windows to view the striking landscape. Here is a perfect hideaway for reading a good book and peace enough for writing one. In more sociable mood, it could be a perfect place to invite friends for a picnic.**

LEFT AND INSET **This simple structure is a perfect contemporary summer house. The interior divides into two areas: one screened by the sliding plywood panels, and another, which includes a sunken bath, screened by horizontal bands of stretched canvas.**

sheds and huts

While it may be among the humblest of buildings – little more than a timber box – the garden shed evokes fond memories for many people. Those lucky enough to have grown up with a garden shed will remember it as the best place for hiding and probably where you were introduced to gardening and growing your first plants. As adults we may just use the shed as storage space, but it can also be transformed into a welcome retreat. It can become a workshop, a hobby den, a place for making wine, a photographic darkroom or even a painting studio. This is a place away from the rules of the home – you are allowed to be untidy and messy and, free from distractions, can become totally absorbed in your endeavours.

There is certainly a great deal of charm in the idea of the garden shed and, if you have space, it is worthwhile experimenting with different designs. Most sheds nowadays are bought from garden centres as modular structures, delivered in a flatpack and assembled on site. You will need a site with a solid concrete base or some sort of platform onto which the structure can be bolted. It is also a very good idea to include an electricity supply for lighting and for power tools or a kettle. In most places, even in protected neighbourhoods such as conservation areas, it is not necessary to seek planning permission for these small, temporary structures. However, as ever, it is worth contacting your planning department to find out the

ABOVE **A modern reworking of the traditional garden shed. The design is a substantial two-bay size and the exterior is finished in a striking blue. The two large porthole windows are like a pair of eyes.**

RIGHT **Much more traditional in style, this rustic shed has a traditional black stained finish on its walls, but with a contrasting pink door. It also has an unusual turf roof. This sort of roof provides high levels of insulation and is also a safe place for wild flowers to flourish.**

local rules and the maximum size of structure permitted.

When the shed is built, think about how it will be fitted out. If it will be used all year, some level of insulation is a good investment. Not only would this make the space more comfortable in winter, it also reduces noise disruption for your neighbours if you use electrical equipment such as power tools or a lathe. Security is a big concern too – any opportunistic thief will know that a shed is likely to be filled with tools and other items of value. So take steps to make sure the doors and windows are secured.

ABOVE **This otherwise tradional-looking shed almost looks as though it has been the victim of a freak tornado and has nose-dived into the garden. A new door has been cut into the roof. This sort of eccentric design is great fun and must surely qualify as a modern folly.**

tree houses

For children and adults alike the tree house is the stuff of dreams. A feature of our imagination from nursery rhymes and children's storybooks from Tarzan to Tolkien, the separate and elevated world of the tree house is a place where anything seems possible.

The tree shelter is familiar to most cultures, not just as an escape from reality but also as a practical hideaway from predators. Tree house origins can be traced back to the Roman emperor Caligula, who is reputed to have held banquets in a huge tree house constructed in a plane tree.

As might be expected, there are practical considerations to take into account when building any tree house. Specialist construction companies begin by assessing whether the chosen tree or trees will be able to support the weight and size of the proposed building. If there is concern about the tree's strength, extra posts can be added to provide support from the ground. Local building regulations will need to be consulted and it is wise to check if the tree is protected by local conservation laws.

The continued health of the tree is also paramount – the aim is to fit the building around the strongest parts of the tree and support it wherever necessary. This can be achieved with brackets and collars and also with bolts. Specialist builders recommend using as few bolts as possible and spacing them at least 45 cm (18 in) apart. Leaving this space between holes reduces the danger of rot.

ABOVE **The contemporary tree house comes in all shapes, sizes and materials. In this case the high-level structure is finished in corrugated metal sheeting and contains a fully plumbed bathroom.**

RIGHT **Here tree house and tree have become so thoroughly entwined it is difficult to tell them apart. This structure is based on a substantial deck – the tree is given extra help to support the weight by the addition of solid corner posts.**

FAR RIGHT **This enigmatic structure is part tree-house and part bird-hide. It is fixed in place between two substantial trees and offers a good vantage point for surveying the surrounding countryside.**

case study – ark tree house

It would be hard to find a more stunning setting for a magical tree house than this secluded wood. Ash and beech trees line the steep sides of the valley and provide the ideal framework for this highly original design, which was the brainchild of a group of six children aged between 3 and 13. The Noah's Ark theme was inspired by a particularly long spell of rainy weather – the children wanted somewhere to play that would be dry and certainly in no danger of flooding. They also wanted their own space for meetings, revising, secret picnics, looking at the stars and getting away from the grown-ups. The tree house was the perfect solution.

The heart of the structure is a simple shed-like building built in pine boards, with great nautical details including porthole windows. There is also plenty of deck space for picnics and to provide a lookout platform. Set slightly apart from the main 'ship' there is an additional platform set into a beech tree and suspended high over the steep valley – this is reached by a wood and rope bridge.

The simplicity of the building, which was built by a former furniture maker who is now a tree house specialist, makes it all the more appealing. The design team decided against filling the interior with furniture, instead choosing soft rugs and cushions.

THE BRIEF: **To design an original tree house for a wooded valley.**

THE SOLUTION: **Inspired by Noah's Ark, this design was moored in a crop of trees with a nearby lookout platform.**

LEFT The tree house is reached by a flight of steps from the bank, but as the land falls away so sharply there is sense of being suspended in mid air when looking out from the far deck.

ABOVE Two large tree trunks climb up through the tree house interior. Collars round the trunks where they emerge through the roof prevent rain from seeping inside.

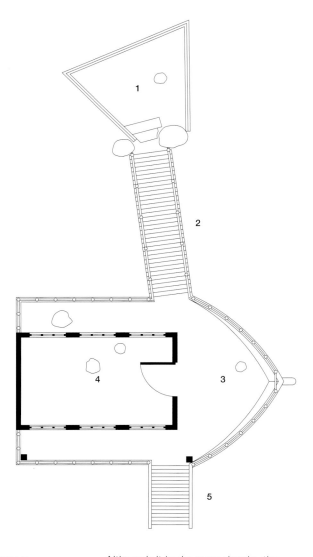

FLOORPLAN
1 viewing deck
2 rope bridge
3 veranda
4 interior
5 steps

Although it looks very simple, the detailing of this project is very special. The prow of the ship is finished with a wavy, thick, rope handrail and a cut-out anchor has been pinned to the side of the boarding. The entrance door has a large porthole to match the others in the side of the cabin. Where the trees poke through the roof there are waterproof collars to prevent rainwater from finding its way inside. There is also a basket-and-pulley-system added to the lookout platform, making it easy to haul up picnics and other essential items.

ABOVE A simple line drawing of the ark tree house, bridge and lookout post shown in position among the copse of trees.

FAR LEFT The prow of the ship or ark is clearly seen here as the tree house 'sails' through the wood. Thoughtful design details include the symbolic anchor, which has been attached to the side and the wavy rope-entwined handrail.

LEFT The extra lookout platform, which is reached by the swaying rope bridge, has its own pulley and hoist. Vital supplies for picnics can be easily hauled up from the valley below.

retreats

ABOVE A simple Oriental style of open-fronted shelter makes an ideal spot for rest and contemplation. It is raised slightly above the garden level to gain better views.

ABOVE RIGHT The simplest of all places to relax and dream, this circle of logs with central table hardly qualifies as a structure, but it is clearly a man-made construction set into the landscape. Retreat spaces close to water are particularly soothing.

RIGHT The Mongolian yurt or ger is a circular structure built from lengths of pliable wood. To keep out the excesses of weather the domed building is covered in layers of thick felt. In really biting cold, layers of animal hides are also used as a covering. Many people find the interiors extremely tranquil, calming spaces.

All the projects featured in this chapter share the common element of being separate from everyday life. That is the key appeal of all spaces we make in our gardens. Here we want a change of tempo, perhaps to enable us to relate more closely with the garden and nature in general, and even to find some spiritual nourishment. The garden retreat, therefore, can be the simplest of spaces, a basic shelter stripped of ornamentation but comfortable enough to rest in quiet.

To decide what sort of retreat you would enjoy or which might be appropriate, the first step is to assess how much space you would like to devote to such a structure. You may have a favourite area of the garden with a great view, a place near a wonderful tree or plant, a corner where the sun falls at the end of the afternoon or a place where you can hear running water or site an artificial pool or water feature. You then need to decide whether you want to create a simple structure – perhaps just a bench with shelter – or something more substantial. For those who chose the very simplest options, think about how and when you would like to visit it – is it a good idea to build in a form of shelter from fierce sunlight or rain?

For those who opt for a more substantial structure there are dozens of ready-to-assemble options available. There is always the reliable garden shed, but if you have more romantic notions of an ideal retreat you could choose from the intriguing and

very beautiful structures evolved by nomadic peoples. Consider a Native American tepee, a long Bedouin tent, a square Berber tent or a circular Mongolian yurt or ger. In each case the shelter has been developed over centuries to meet the needs of its inhabitants – for example, the yurt can provide warmth even in Arctic temperatures and is cool in summer, it can be dismantled and packed up into a bundle and it can be re-erected in just half an hour.

Building materials, furnishings and colours are absolutely crucial to making a structure that is sympathetic to the need for a restful, peaceful, natural place. Most of the nomadic structures mentioned above are built around a wooden pole frame and then draped with a type of canvas or wool felt that keeps out wind and rain. In a very wet climate there is a danger of rot and mould, so it may be wise to pack up during the worst winter months.

If you decide that you would prefer to design your retreat, you could commission an architect to help you realise your dream. Some unusual recent projects have included sculptural shelters, almost like caves, built using rubble and earth, and even entire structures made from woven willow that is rooted in the ground, later becoming a living shelter. Interestingly in almost every culture, these structures are based on soft, curved shapes that appear to embrace the occupants.

working in the garden

For increasing numbers of people working at home either part or full time is now a reality. For this you need a quiet place, ideally somewhere distinct from the main part of the home – somewhere to retreat when work beckons. Where space is limited inside, the garden has become an ideal location for a home office. Many people actually prefer to work in a place separate from the home so that there is a sense of going out to work; being away from the hub of home life also reduces the distractions.

However, to make an outside office requires more than just setting up a desk in a shed. If you are going to take your work seriously and earn a living, then the office environment should also be taken seriously. In some cases it will be possible to convert an existing building such as a garage or a large shed. Alternatively, there are growing numbers of companies specializing in making freestanding offices and workshops.

The first design consideration is size – don't work in a cramped space, and allow room for expansion. Next comes comfort – make sure the insulation is of a high standard, that there is plenty of natural light and that you have good-quality furnishings, particularly a large desk and ergonomic chair. Then install the best possible services – electricity is a must, but also think about a couple of phone lines or a fast internet connection. Water is a good idea, too – being able to make a cup of coffee and perhaps including a lavatory and/or shower in the design will all help to make work more enjoyable. Finally, make sure the place is secure from intruders.

LEFT & BELOW This converted grain silo looks completely at home in its rural setting. Inside the space contains a well-equipped home office. The use of natural materials, such as untreated wood planking to line the walls and floor, makes this a particularly healthy and inspiring work environment.

FAR LEFT This is an ingenious reworking of a disused garage. The substantial brick building at the bottom of this townhouse garden has been converted into a welcoming home office. Inside there are even such thoughtful details as a lavatory and a small kitchen for making hot drinks and snacks.

case study –
the whim

There is something about small buildings in a woodland setting that is highly evocative of fairy tales – Hansel and Gretel, Little Red Riding Hood and more besides. This compact and fantastical structure in the wooded corner of an American garden is exactly in that mould. Appropriately enough it has the wistful name of The Whim.

While the architect owner originally thought the new structure might become a meditation space or a chapel, and it could easily be used as a home office or workshop, in fact The Whim has been designed as a tiny retreat and guest lodge. From the outside the cosy hideaway is clad from its crown-shaped chimney top to the ground in dark grey cedar shingles. Around the top of the wall is a band of small rectangular fixed windows rather like a church clerestory, while at first floor level there are standard, off-the-shelf, natural wood opening windows.

Inside the irregularly shaped conical structure, the high-ceilinged space contains a place to sleep, a miniature kitchen, bathroom, and a seating area with an extremely efficient Finnish-made, wood-burning stove that is able to heat up the space very quickly.

The Whim stands on a base with a small area of timber deck, and it is as much a piece of furniture as a building. It was constructed by a carpenter, but because the shape is not an ordinary cone – it tapers and is not strictly geometric – it was certainly a challenge

ABOVE The entrance to The Whim is found tucked neatly into the space where the conical body of the building joins the small bathroom lean-to.

RIGHT The building has a fairy tale quality, clearly not a house, but much more than a shed or den. Its complex shape gives it enormous charm.

to build. Just about every piece had to be measured and cut individually, and each of the dark grey shingles on the exterior had to be cut by hand.

The entire structure is made from wood, both inside and out. The roof and exterior walls are covered with cedar shingles and the windows are standard, off-the-shelf designs. Inside the finish uses birch plywood, and the millwork is of maple. The flooring of limestone was quarried not far away at a site near the Mississippi River. The owners requested high levels of insulation to be built in to cope with

THE BRIEF: To make a small, but very cosy guest house for year-round use.

THE SOLUTION: A fairy tale structure of irregular shape and enormous character.

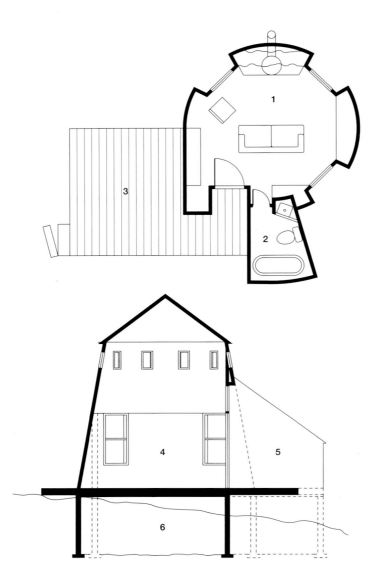

FLOORPLAN
1 living/bedroom
2 bathroom
3 deck

CROSS SECTION
4 living/bedroom
5 bathroom
6 ground

the severe climate. This now ensures that even in the harshest winter the interior remains warm and cosy.

The interior space is like a scaled down cathedral, or perhaps a tepee. The architect was inspired by tepee building since the area has a long history of use by Native Americans. It is possible to interpret the vertical

strips of dark wood perhaps as the supports for a tepee structure. These dark lines also create the illusion of extra height and draw the eye up to the ceiling.

Despite the simplicity of its materials, this is a retreat with all the comforts of home. There is an electrical supply and running water.

ABOVE The interior floor space measures just 19.5 m² (210 ft²), but there is room enough for two people to enjoy a restful retreat with great views of the garden along with the comforts of running water and an area for cooking simple meals.

LEFT The roof concludes in this irregular starburst-pattern on the ceiling which the architect describes as the 'Eye of God'. The band of windows at the top of the wall lets light flood into the interior.

now

By the time you have reached this stage of the book, I hope you are filled with ideas and inspiration for ways of adding more space to your home. This chapter is devoted to tackling the planning and building of the work and ensuring that your grand plans can be transformed into a real structure.

First, be sure that you have made the right decision, that you like where you live and are prepared to lavish time and money on improvements. If so are you prepared to go through the mess and disruption of building works? If it is a major addition, you might consider moving out for a while.

Are you confident that you are adding space in the right places and that you will end up with genuinely useful changes to your home? Be bold – make sure your ideas will not just add value to your home but will also improve the quality of space and your quality of life.

Here follows a practical step-by-step guide to deciding where and how to add more space, what practicalities you need to consider and how to research and choose the best possible architect and builder for the job.

LEFT **While this initially appears to be a contemporary house, the original structure on this site dates back to the nineteenth century and the original basement has been incorporated into the new design. On close inspection, house detectives will also find that deep inside the new shell there lurks a remodelled and extended 1950s house.**

drawing up your plans

With lots of ideas and options in mind, now is the time to translate dreams into reality. The first step is to identify your reasons for adding more space. Because few of us have the luxury of designing and building our own home, we are left to use our resources to make the most of the home we have. Perhaps you have just moved to a place with potential for expansion or alterations to suit the way you live or you may have lived in the same place for a while and need to make changes because of new circumstances. Perhaps a partner has moved in and your living space feels cramped, you are planning to work from home, or you need to make room for a baby or lodger or create a guest space. Whatever the reason, ask yourself some basic questions before getting started on any building project. Are you honestly happy with the property and its location? Is it convenient for work, transportation, family and friends? If you are unsure, it is worth taking a look at some of the properties for sale through estate agents both locally and in other areas. You might be surprised by what you can get for your money and realize that lavishing more on your present home will be money unwisely spent. Even if you're certain that an extension or conversion is the best option, it is still well worthwhile taking a look round a few similarly improved homes for sale. You can borrow ideas and gauge whether you like what other people have achieved in similar properties.

If you are happy with your present home, be sure that it is worth spending a large sum on improvements. Will this add value to the property and enhance your enjoyment of the place and, most important of all, will it improve your quality of life?

The next step is to decide just how and where to add your extra space. A garden-level extension offers a highly flexible area if you need to expand your living space – ideal for making room for a home office, extending the kitchen or adding a tranquil space that overlooks the garden. A two-storey extension opens up the opportunities for an extra bathroom, bedroom, study or guest room, while an attic conversion proves ideal for a whole range of uses from a new family living room or quiet office to a playroom or teenage hideaway. However, as illustrated elsewhere in this book, the project doesn't have to be huge to make a big difference – a small balcony outside a bedroom can transform the interior space, even if it provides only just enough room for a chair to sit on and enjoy the sun. Equally, by covering over the side passageway of a terrace house, you suddenly have the opportunity to completely revise and re-plan the ground floor living space.

RIGHT **An intriguing mixture of traditional brickwork with glass and steel makes this an exciting light-filled extension. The pale stone floor tiles can be easily swept clean. Glass doors lead into the garden.**

turning ideas into reality

Once you have decided where you would most like to add more space, the next step is to consider how that space will look and feel. If you are planning to build an extension, think about how much room would be useful. Of course this will be dictated partly by budget, but you also need to take into account the proportions of your existing home. A tiny addition might not provide enough extra space to be worth the disruption and expense, while a vast extension may look oddly out of proportion with the rest of the building. However, thinking small is not necessarily a bad thing – sometimes the addition of something as modest as an extra loo or shower

room can ease the family morning and evening rush hour, or can add a touch of luxury to a bedroom.

At the same time, start to consider how the new space will look, both inside and out. If you are planning an extension do you want it to be entirely in sympathy with the rest of the building and therefore constructed of similar materials, or do you want extra space that has a personality of its own such as a high-tech all-glass box? An extension clad in wood or hung with slate tiles will make an interesting addition, and may complement or contrast with the existing structure. Balconies can look fabulous in all sorts of materials – don't feel obliged to

follow tradition, but consider a steel frame with canvas sides and wood decking or a wrought-iron structure with glass panels.

If you are digging into a basement or cellar then windows and doors will be big considerations and you will probably want to include as much glass as possible. Think about what style of doors and windows would appeal most: consider doors that slide open and shut, concertina doors that fold right back out of view or huge panels of glass that are pivoted to swing horizontally or vertically.

This is the moment to consider whether it is worth spending extra on double- or triple-glazing, whether you need to include toughened glass as protection from intruders and whether you need additional security features such as metal bars or an upgraded alarm system. It might also be the time to think about incorporating solar technologies such as photovoltaics – these are cells that can be incorporated into glass or roof tiles to help produce your own supply of clean solar power.

If you would prefer your building materials to be environmentally friendly, you could use salvaged and recycled materials, or make sure that materials such as hardwoods have come from sustainably managed sources. A good-quality builder's merchant will be able to tell you where its timber comes from. There are also growing numbers of builder's merchants who specialize in

ecologically sound products from timbers through to paints.

And finally think about the quality of the internal space. How do you want it to feel – indistinguishable from the existing house or with a completely separate personality? Introvert and cosy or extrovert and open plan? Will it have a traditional or modern feel? Will the ceilings be high or low; the walls curved or straight? Think about the finishings: will you have hard flooring such as stone or ceramic tiles, or something softer such as timber, sisal or wool carpet? Take these last decisions into account when planning a colour scheme that reflects the use and personality of the new room.

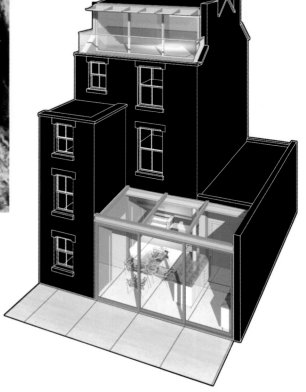

LEFT The architecture practice that worked on this attic conversion raised the roof to make a large open-plan living area.

ABOVE Computer-generated images help architects to convey the ideas in their designs. Software programmes can be used to create a 'walk-through' of the proposed home before building work begins.

RIGHT This is another style of computer-generated design. In this case there is an exciting rear addition to the roof and a glass and steel back extension containing a kitchen and dining area.

practicalities up front

The one absolutely vital task in any building project is to work out the extent of your budget. Decide how much you can afford to spend, how much you have in savings and how much your lender will provide and whether you can afford to keep up with the repayments. Establish a realistic budget and stick to it.

With a figure very firmly fixed in your mind, it's time to find out if your budget can meet your dreams. Building work is expensive – you will be paying for a whole range of services, materials and skills – but if you have chosen wisely, your spend should convert into an investment and add to the value of your property. To put this in context, it now costs the price of a small car to move house, so if you have decided to stay and improve rather than to move, the expenditure is well worthwhile.

Whatever the budget and however confident you are in the skills of your architect and builder, always build in a contingency sum of money, just in case. Once building work starts it may reveal all sorts of unexpected problems. You may find your foundations need underpinning, or a stripped roof may expose an unexpected amount of rotten rafters. During rewiring you may discover that the entire system needs an overhaul. These sorts of set backs do not happen in every job, but it is far better to be prepared with extra cash if necessary. Opinions differ about how large a contingency or emergency

fund should be. On a small, simple job reserve around 15% of the total costs; on large, complex works, it is sensible to increase that to at least 20%.

With the budget in place, you will next have to consider planning permission. If your home is in a protected historic building you may find that your ambitions to extend up, down or out will be severely curtailed. If the home is in a protected historic neighbourhood as well, there are even more severe limitations imposed on what you can do to alter your home. There have been occasions when owners have been refused permission to change a single item on the exterior of their home – their only option to gain more space was to excavate under the entire house and add a whole new basement level. Your local planning authority will be able to advise on restrictions.

However, free from the hindrance of heritage, there are still hurdles to be leapt. Adding almost any sort of extension will require planning permission from the local authority. It will need to be satisfied that the proposals are safe and sound and the neighbours will have to be consulted.

Handling neighbours often requires sensitivity. People don't like to be surprised with official notices appearing on the street proclaiming that major building works are under consideration. The best approach is to talk to people at the early stages of your ideas, describe your plans and show some sketches.

Your project budget will need to cover the following:

- architect's fee
- planning fees
- construction costs from builder
- plumber, electrician and gas engineer
- new doors and windows
- glazier and carpenter
- flooring
- decorating
- bathroom or kitchen fittings
- contingency sum of at least 15% in case of disaster

At this stage the final point to consider is whether the structure of your home is suited to your plans. For example, if you are considering adding an extra storey on top of a house, make sure the foundations are solid and that the walls can carry the extra weight – this is a job for a structural engineer. You may also need to check the foundations if you are adding an extension. Many older properties are built on shallow rubble and so adding an extension will also require

considerable reinforcing of those meagre foundations. For those wanting to convert an attic, the roof struts need to be designed in such a way to make conversion possible. And finally, if the project is shaping up to be extremely disruptive, now is the time to decide whether you can live in a building site (it will be messier and more disagreeable than you think). You may want to take the opportunity to live with friends or rent somewhere nearby for the duration.

ABOVE **Although it looks perfectly at home as part of this mansion block's roof structure, this stylish room with its light-filled interior is, in fact, a prefabricated extension. The structure was made in a factory and then carefully hoisted by crane into place at the top of the building.**

LEFT **The large window opening sits next to the corner turret of this characterful apartment block. The prefabricated structure slots back into the roof and now makes a luxury penthouse apartment.**

getting to grips with plans

before

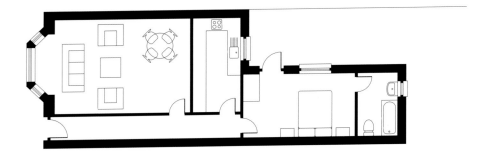

after

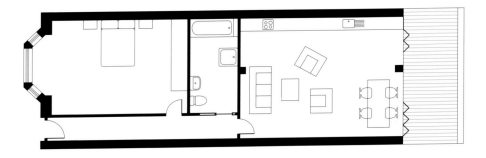

ABOVE **Among the many skills that architects have to offer is that of space engineering. The best architects can visit a badly designed home and immediately make suggestions for improving the use of space and circulation between rooms. In the case above, a small side extension succeeds in unlocking the congested plan and opens the flat onto a deck and into the garden. The quality of the new-look home environment is improved immeasurably.**

By this stage you will probably have amassed piles of paper covered in sketches. I find it useful very early in a project to make my own measured drawings, which help to firm up ideas. These don't have to be meticulous, but measuring your existing rooms gives you a real feel for the spaces. I measure just about everything – walls and floors obviously, but also the height and width of doors and the positions of electrical sockets. There are plenty of excellent computer programmes available for this type of task – try those, too.

All of this preliminary work is extremely useful in helping to imagine and visualize the project. Photocopies of your own drawings make it possible to experiment with reordering the spaces. Try swapping a bedroom and a kitchen to see how this affects the flow of the spaces. What difference could it make if you remove the wall of a hallway and integrate that space into a living room? However, before plans can be approved officially and work is under way, these sketches and ideas need to be formalized and converted into technical drawings. This is a job for the project architect or a suitably qualified draftsperson.

Professionally executed plans perform a number of functions. From these the planning authorities can be reassured that the proposed works meet building requirements, you will know exactly what you are getting for your money and the builder will have a blueprint for the work to be carried out. Plans are absolutely vital in letting everyone know exactly what is going on. You may have requested a gap between a window and door to be large enough for a piece of furniture or asked for doors and windows to line up in a way that gives you a great view over the garden – it only takes a miscalculation of centimetres to spoil those ideas. With a plan you have a document which leaves no room for misunderstanding or argument.

There are two basic types of technical drawings – the three-dimensional and two-dimensional. The

BELOW **This vertical slice through a property is called the cross-section. In this drawing it is easy to identify key elements such as the doors and stairs.**

RIGHT **Two floor plans show the layout of rooms as they might be seen from above. A floor plan is a horizontal slice through a property. Once again it is easy to spot main features such as the stairs, bathroom suite, kitchen units and doors.**

first floor

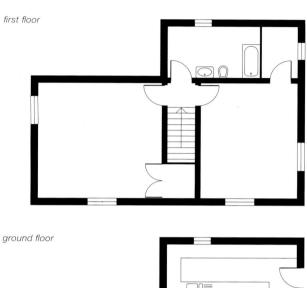

cross-section

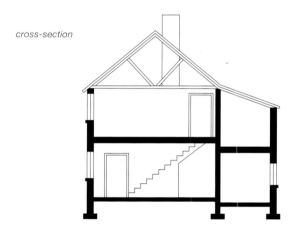

ground floor

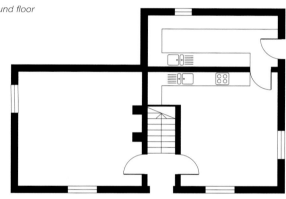

first type is hardest to draw, but it does reveal very clearly how building spaces relate to each other. The two-dimensional drawing comes in three versions – the floor plan, which is a horizontal slice through a building looking down on the floor layout; the cross-section, which is a vertical slice through the space showing rooms from side on; and the elevation, which looks at the outside of a building from the front, back or sides.

When it comes to 'reading' and understanding these plans, the first step is to find a familiar landmark – the

front door or staircase, perhaps – and then work out the sequence spaces from that point. Technical drawings should include as many details as possible, such as markings for doorways (and which way the door hangs), windows, chimneys and other structural features. It is also a good idea to mark items such as electrical sockets and switches, and perhaps any other services including known water pipes and radiators. The more information you have, the better you will be to make decisions. For example, in an attic conversion you

may have decided very early on where you would like to put a bed or sofa. That should be included on the plans so that the central-heating engineers don't put a radiator in the way.

In fact, you may discover that your architect has a couple of sets of plans, including one specifically for services including central heating and electrical wiring. I always recommend taking your own photocopies of the plans so that you can add in useful details. You might also map in large items of furniture like a bed or a table to give the space a sense of scale.

working with an architect and builder

Taking on any sort of building project is time consuming, nerve racking, messy, stressful, exhausting and expensive. That said, it is also incredibly exciting and can become thoroughly absorbing. It is a great feeling to watch your plans being transformed from paper sketches to a whole new three-dimensional space. Because of the complexities and potential for problems in building projects, I strongly recommend using an architect for any extensions or remodelling jobs.

For many years the architectural profession has suffered from a poor public image. The stereotype is that they are arrogant, uptight and absolutely determined to pursue their own vision regardless of the pleas of the client. They are also often seen as an expensive luxury. Of course, every profession has its difficult characters, but if every architect behaved so badly, how would they ever make a living? In recent years, that stereotype has shown real signs of disappearing. The new generation of architects has produced ideas that have captured the public's imagination and many design teams are more willing than ever to take on domestic work. I have endless admiration for many architects who have tremendous skills at visualizing a whole project, homing in on the problems and offering quite brilliant solutions. Many also know excellent builders and have great ideas about what materials to use, and the finished work can add significant value to your property. But it is not only the

profession that has changed; the public has also undergone a transformation from being fairly conservative and nostalgia-loving to clients prepared to commission adventurous designs.

The choice of architect is absolutely key to a successful job. It must be a relationship of trust and respect. You are handing over your home, a big budget and your potential future happiness. Finding the right architect takes time and patience. In most countries the professional body will provide a service with a shortlist of potential candidates. Those selected should have worked on similar projects. Alternatively, you can visit your local architecture centre or collect names and recommendations from friends and neighbours.

With a shortlist of perhaps half a dozen, make a preliminary phone call to ask some basic questions. Do the architects work in your area, do they carry out the sort of work you are planning and do they have time to fit in with your plans? From an initial conversation it should be possible to make a list of three to talk to in more detail. Visit their offices, ask to see photographs of previous projects and show them some sketch ideas and perhaps photographs of your home. Give a general idea of the budget and

RIGHT **Many architects have a vast knowledge of interesting materials. In this project it is clear that every item from the blonde wood flooring to the glass panelled walls has been chosen with extreme care.**

see how they respond. If you like what you see and you establish a rapport you are well on the way to finding your architect. I would also suggest visiting previous jobs and talking to clients. Ask them about the process, whether the timetable was accurate, whether the budget was adhered to and what, if any, were the major problems. Establish whether they would consider using the architect again and would recommend him or her. You can't predict exactly how you will get on, but by doing your research and asking plenty of questions, you should be able to avoid the worst mistakes.

Remember, this is not a relationship to rush into. One useful test is to ask yourself whether you would be happy to go for lunch or for a drink with the architect, and whether you are confident that you will get the results you want. If it helps, you could ask the candidates to visit your property and suggest a couple of design ideas. While initial meetings are free of charge, you should expect to pay for this extra service, so make sure you are clear about what you want and how much it will cost. Ask what fees will be charged for the whole job – sometimes this will be a fixed price, but most often it will be a percentage of the whole building cost. Check whether there will be extra charges for tax, office expenses and travelling to and from site, and finally establish whether or not the whole project will be adequately covered by their insurance policy.

The architect must be able to get on with you, too. Always be truthful; if you don't like something, then say so immediately. If you don't understand plans ask them to be explained, and if you are working to an extremely tight budget, say so right at the start. The longer you leave things and the less you communicate, the more difficult the process becomes. Clarify early on exactly what the architect's role will be. This can range from drawing plans and submitting them to the local council for approval through to completion, or may only mean taking charge of single elements such as producing drawings. If you are undertaking a project with a partner or friend make sure you are in complete agreement – if not, you are only storing up trouble for yourself later should anything go wrong.

Once you have made your choice of designer, plans can be discussed in more detail and you can start to think about builders. The choice of builder comes when plans are underway and the architect has prepared a schedule of works, listing every stage of work to be undertaken. Even if you know a very good builder, it is a good idea to see whom the architect suggests, too. It is usual for two or three builders to provide a quote based on the schedule of works. Don't automatically opt for the cheapest – it may be that the most expensive option will provide the best-quality job. In the same way that you shortlisted and researched the architect, do the same again for the builder.

Once again, visit previous clients and look at the work. Ask questions to reassure yourself you are making the right choice – did the builders keep to the time schedule, were they friendly and trustworthy, and did they turn up when they said they would and work regular hours? Did they play loud music or double-park outside in the street and block in the neighbours? Were they careful about the rest of the home? Finding good builders is a challenge and the very best are worth their weight in gold. If you have particular concerns, talk them through right at the start of the job – it can be incredibly difficult to raise criticisms and concerns half-way through. Some questions might include what hours they expect to work, how many people will be on site at any one time and how many people will hold keys to the premises. Discuss whether they hang plastic sheeting to protect the rest of the house from dust, how much equipment and materials will be needed on site and whether they regularly clean up after themselves and so on. This should also be discussed with the architect, since he or she will be overseeing the building works.

When you feel confident that your questions have been answered and that your mind is at ease you can begin to think about signing a contract.

RIGHT **Taking time to find the right builders and architect is always time well spent, particularly if you are planning an unusual or finely detailed project, such as this pretty garden pavilion.**

address book

UK ARCHITECTS

51% Studios
1–5 Clerkenwell Road,
London EC1M 5PA
T: 020 7251 6963
www.51pct.com

The Architects Practice
23 Beacon Hill,
London N7 9LY
T: 020 7607 3333
www.architects-
practice.com

Alan Philips Architects
Unit 4 Level 4,
New England House,
New England Street,
Brighton BN1 4GH
T: 01273 626276

Azman Owens
1 St Peter's Street,
Islington, London N18JD
T: 020 7354 2955

Brookes Stacey Randall
16 Winchester Walk,
London SE1 9AG
T: 020 7403 0707
www.bsr-architects.com

Burd Haward Marston
The Old School,
Exton Street,
London SE1 8UE
T: 020 7401 7770

Cantos Bailey Architects
Studio 11, Tiger House,
Burton Street, London
WC1H 9BY
T: 020 7388 7337
www.cantosbailey.com

Charles Barclay
74 Josephine Avenue,
London SW2 2LA
T: 020 8674 0037

Cowan Architects
9–10 Old Stone Link,
Ship Street, East Grinstead,
West Sussex RH19 4EF
T: 01342 410242

**Cullum and Nightingale
  Architects**
61 Judd Street,
London WC1H 9QT
T: 020 7383 4466
www.cn-architects.co.uk

Diane Williams Architect
Whingate, Whinacres,
Conway, LL32 8ET
Tel: 01492 593480

Derek Wylie Architecture
241–251 Ferndale Road,
London SW9 8BJ
T: 020 7274 6373
www.studio-dwa.co.uk

Donnelly & O'Neill
41 Fitzwilliam Street,
Belfast BT9 6AW
T: 028 9032 1824

**FAT (Fashion Architecture
Taste)**
116–120 Golden Lane,
London EC1Y OTF
T: 020 7251 6735

Form Design Architecture
1 Bermondsey Exchange
179–181 Bermondsey
Street, London SE1 3UW
T: 020 7407 3336
www.form-
architecture.co.uk

Harrison Ince Architects
2 Jordan Street, Knott Mill,
Manchester M15 4PY
T: 0161 236 3650Littman

Helen Dye
167a Queens Road,
Tunbridge Wells,
Kent TN4 9JX
T:01892 547767

**Hugh Pilkington
  Architects**
Richmond House,
Orford, Suffolk IP12 2BU
T: 01394 450102

**Littman Goddard Hogarth
  Architects**
12 Chelsea Wharf,
15 Lots Road,
London SW10 0QJ
T: 020 7351 7871
www.lgh-architect.co.uk

Loates-Taylor Shannon
1 Blue Line Place,
237 Long Lane,
London SE1 4PZ
T: 020 7357 7000
www.lts-architects.co.uk

**London Basement
  Company**
Unit B, Innovation House,
292 Worton Road,
Isleworth, TW7 6EL
T: 020 8847 9449

Loyn & Co Architects
21 Victoria Road,
Penarth CF64 3EG
T: 029 2071 1432

m3
74 Great Eastern Street,
London EC2A 3JG
T: 020 7724 4222
www.m3architects.com

McCaren Design
Floor 3, 26 Lockyer Street,
Plymouth, Devon PL1 2QW
T: 01752 209417

Neil Choudhury Architects
132 Southwark Street,
London SE1 0SW
T: 020 7633 9933

Pear Tree (Treehouses)
The Stables,
Mansheugh Rd, Fenwick,
Ayrshire, KA3 6AN
T: 01560 600111

Proctor:Rihl
63 Cross Street,
Islington, London N1 2BB
T: 020 7704 6003

Seth Stein
Grand Union Central
    West Row,
London W10 5AS
T: 020 8968 8581

Simon Conder
8 Nile Street, London N1 7RF
T: 020 7251 2144

Stan Bolt Architect
The Old Museum,
Higher Street, Brixham,
Devon TQ5 8HW
T: 01803 852588

Studio MG
101 Turnmill Street,
London EC1M 5QP
T: 020 7251 2648

Theis and Khan
    Architects
22a Batemans Row,
London E2A 3HH
T: 020 7729 9329

Thomas de Cruz
    Architects/Designers
80/82 Chiswick High Road,
London W4 1SY
T: 020 8995 8100
www.thomasdecruz.com

Zombory-Moldovan
    Moore Architects
25b Underwood Street,
London N1 7LG
T: 020 7251 8888

EURO ARCHITECTS
Eduard Böhtlingk
Herenstraat 40,
Postbus 80 3155 ZH,
Maasland, Netherlands
T: +31 10 591 4807
www.bohtlingk.nl

Entasis Arkitekter
Magstraede 10 c 2,
1204 Copenhagen,
Denmark
T: +45 3333 9525

Jarmund/Vigsnaes
Kristian Augusts Gate 11,
0164 Oslo, Norway
T: +47 22 994 343

Ronny d'Hespeel
    Architect
Lange Raamstraat 18,
8000 Bruges, Netherlands
T: +31 50 33 02 85

Soren Robert Lund
    Associates
St Kongensgade 110E,
1264 Coperhagen,
Denmark
T: +45 33 91 01 00

Stephane Beel
Koningin Astridiaan 7/19,
8200 Bruges
Belgium
T: +32 50 30 19 50

Studio Archea
Via della Fornace 30/R,
50125 Florence, Italy
T: +39 055 685 202

ASIA / US / AUSTRALIA
ARCHITECTS
Belmont Freeman
    Architects
110 West 40th Street,
Suite 2401, New York,
NY 10018 US
T: +1 212 382 3311

Engelen Moore
44 McLachlan Avenue,
Rushcutters Bay,
Sydney 2011, Australia
T: +61 2 9380 4099

Hanrahan Meyers
    Architects
22 West 21st Street,
New York, NY 10010 US
T: +1 212 989 6026

McBride Charles Ryan
4/21 Wynnstay Road
Praham
Victoria
Australia 3181
T: +61 3 95 101 006

Olson Sundberg
108 1st Avenue South,
Seattle, Washington
98104, US
T: +1 206 624 5670

Stageberg Beyer Sachs
115 4th Avenue North,
Minneapolis, MN 55401, US
T: +1 612-375-1399

Stephen Varady
363A Pitt Street,
Sydney, NSW 2000,
Australia
T: +61 2 9283 6880

Tadao Ando
5–23 Toyosaki 2-Chome,
Kita-ku, Osaka 531-0072,
Japan
T: +81 6 6375 1148

Tsao & McKown
20 Vandam Street,
New York, NY 10013, US
T: +1 212 337 3800

Wendell Burnette
9830 North 17th Street,
Phoenix, Arizona, US
T: +1 602 395 1091

Wesley Wei Architects
100 North 3rd Street,
Philadelphia,
Pennsylvania 19106, US
T: +1 215 592 8118

index

Page numbers in *italic* refer
to illustrations

acknowledgements

The publisher would like to thank the following photographers and architects for their kind permission to reproduce the photographs in this book:

1 Ross Honeysett (Wayne Davies Architects); 2–3 Roos Aldershoff (Architect:Eduard Bohtlingk); 4 left Andrew Twort (MMM Architects); 4 right Nicholas Kane (Theis & Khan Architects); 4 centre Nicholas Kane/Arcaid (Theis & Khan Architects); 5 left Dennis Gilbert/View (Simon Knox Architects); 5 right Richard Davies; 5 centre Graf Luckner/Camera Press; 6–7 Clive Frost; 8 Andrew Twort (MMM Architects); 10 Matthew Anrobus/National Trust Photo Library; 10–11 Catherine Bogert (Wesley Wei Architects); 12 left Fay Sweet; 12 right Fritz Von Der Schulenberg/The Interior Archive; 13 Rupert Truman/National Trust Photo Library; 14 and 15 below John Gollings (Bird de La Coeur Architects); 16–17 Peter Durant/arcblue.com; 18 Dennis Gilbert/View (Chance De Silva Architects); 19 Christian Richters; 20 Richard Moore/Knight Frank Kensington Office; 20–21 Richard Bryant/Arcaid (Seth Stein Architects); 22 James Harris (Architects: Ushida Findlay); 23 Grazzi Branco/Iketrade; 24 Jerry Harpur (Design: Juan Grimm, Chile); 25 Tim Street–Porter/Esto; 26 Nigel Young (Architects:Foster and Partners); 27 Keith Paisley (FAT Architects); 28 Nicholas Kane/Arcaid (Theis & Khan Architects); 30 Ray Main/Mainstream; 31 Jean–Francois Jaussaud (Architects: Simon Conder Associates); 32 Paul Ryan/International Interiors (Designer: Miki Astori); 33 Grazzi Branco/Iketrade; 34 Henry Wilson/The Interior Archive (Designer: Michael Reeves); 35 Grazzi Branco/Iketrade; 36–39 Giulio Oriani/Vega MG; 40 Mike Neale (Form Design Architecture); 40–41 Sue Barr (Architects: 51% Studios Ltd); 42 Tim Beddow/The Interior Archive (Architect: Garrett O'Hayan); 43 above and below: Nicholas Kane (Architects: Buschow Henley); 44 Michael Moran (Architects: Sage Winter Coombe); 44–45 Verne Fotografie; 45 Sinisa Savic (Charles Barclay Architects); 46 Fritz Von der Schulenberg/The Interior Archive; 47 Simon Archer (Architects: Simon Conder Associates); 48–51 Mark Luscombe–Whyte (Architects: Simon Conder Associates); 52 Deidi von Schaewen; 52–53 Andrea Jones; 53 below Marianne Majerus (Design: Diana Yakeley Associates Ltd); 54 Marianne Majerus (Design: Michèle Osborne/Panorama Landscape Design); 55 Elizabeth Whiting & Associates; 56 Guy Obijn; 57 Verne Fotografie (Architects: Sky Studios); 58 Bieke Claessens (Stylist: Kristel Joossen); 58 right Jerry Harpur (Designer: Terence Conran); 59 Deidi von Schaewen; 60–63 Mitsuo Matsuoka (Tadao Ando Architects); 64 Nicholas Kane (Theis & Khan Architects); 66 left Gross and Daley; 66 right and 67 David Churchill (Stickland Coombe Architects); 68 Ray Main/ Mainstream (Architects: Loates Taylor Shannon); 69 Paul Avis (Architects: Loates Taylor Shanon); 70–71 Ray Main/Mainstream (Architect: Loates Taylor Shannon); 72 Charlotte Wood (Architects: Cullum & Nightingale); 73 Richard Glover/View (Reading and West Architects); 74 left Deidi von Schaewen; 74–75 Grazzi Branco/Iketrade; 75 Elizabeth Whiting & Associates; 76 John Freeman (Design: Brian Muller); 77 David George (Crawford & Gray Architects); 78–81 Ray Main/Mainstream (Architect: Martin Lee Associates); 82–83 Richard Moore/ Knight Frank Kensington Office; 84–87 Winfried Heinze/Conran Octopus (Interior Designer: Clare Rutland, Furniture Designer: James Sugden/ London Basement Company); 88 Dennis Gilbert/View (Simon Knox Architects); 90 David Brittain (Architect:Hugh Pilkington); 91 left Dennis Gilbert/View (Sonya Polescuk Architects); 91 right Peter Durant/arcblue.com (Alan Philips Architects); 92 Glen Lowlock (The Architects Practice); 92–93 Chris Gascoigne/View (Architects: Simon Conder Associates); 93 Fay Sweet; 94–97 Morley von Sternberg (Architects: Burd Howard Marston); 98 Kim Sayer/Red Cover; 98–99 Marcus Hilton (Roland Cowan Architects); 100 David Grandorge (Zombory–Moldovan Moore Architects); 101 Ian Fussell (Architect:Cantos Bailey); 102–103 Edmund Sumner (Architects: Martin Burton and Michael Casey); 103 above Edmund Sumner (Architect: Michael Casey); 103 below Edmund Sumner (Architect: Martin Burton); 104 105 Mike Neale (Form Design Architecture) 106 Nicola Browne; 106–107 Camera Press; 108–109 Peter Clarke (McBride Charles Ryan); 110–111 Trevor Mein (McBride Charles Ryan); 112 Ken Hayden/Red Cover; 113 Marianne Majerus(Design: Michèle Osborne/Panorama Landscape Design/ Architect: (Walters & Cohen); 114 left Ken Hayden/Red Cover (Andrei Zarzycki); 114–115 Deidi von Schaewen; 115 Jerry Harpur (Tom Carruth and John Furman, LA); 116–117 Ken Hayden/Red Cover (Architect: John Pawson); 117 Nigel Noyes (Architect: Scott Weston); 118–121 Charlotte Wood (Architect: Cullum & Nightingale); 122 Graf Luckner/Camera Press; 124–125 Heiner Orth/ Architectur & Wohnen; 126 Giulio Oriana/Vega MG; 127 left Dennis Gilbert/View (Edward Cullinan Architects); 127 right Jerry Harpur (John Holmes, Sonoma, CA); 128 Mark Burgin/Arcaid (Architect: Gabriel Poole); 128–129 Richard Waite; 129 Elizabeth Whiting & Associates; 130–133 Chris Tubbs/Red Cover; 134 left Elizabeth Whiting & Associates; 134 right Nicola Browne; 135 Gavin Kingcome/ Gardens Illustrated; 136 Nicholas Kane/Arcaid (Theis & Khan Architects); 136–137 Klauss Ott (Eberhand Stauss); 138–141 Dana Wheelock (James Stageberg Architects/Parallel Lines); 142 Richard Davies; 144–145 Dennis Gilbert/View (Design: Antenna); 146 Mike Neale (Form Design Architecture); 147 M3 Architects (Graphics–M3 FX); 148–149 Nicholas Kane/Arcaid; 152–153 Peter Cook/View (Architects: Patel Taylor); 155 Viv Yeo/Narratives (Eger Architects)

Every effort has been made to trace the copyright holders, architects and designers. We apologise in advance for any unintentional omission and would be pleased to insert the appropriate acknowledgment in any subsequent additions.